Bob Ross

THE CALM AND WISDOM OF THE BELOVED PAINTER

Contents

Bob was committed to keeping painting accessible—to getting great effect without using any fancy tools.

WHY WE LOVE BOB ROSS

by Jim Needham

In 1981, a tall, lanky patriot finished his service in the Air Force and began to paint himself into the American Story.

Bob Ross showed up unannounced at our station one day in the winter of 1983 to pitch an idea for a painting show. As the general manager of WIPB-TV in Muncie, Indiana, I had the privilege of meeting him and his business partner Annette Kowalski when they visited. We went to lunch, talked over their dreams and the program they wanted us to record and distribute, signed the contract, and rolled on with the project. It was as easy as that. We knew immediately that *The Joy of Painting* would be something special.

Bob worked with us for ten years producing the show, eventually moving to Muncie in the late 80's to be closer to the station. Regardless of the distractions of travel and guest appearances across the county as his show gathered its audience, Bob recorded thirteen shows every three months and our partnership thrived under his friendship and professionalism. He had a rare and unpredictable sense of humor, an inspiring optimism, and a crystal-clear vision about what he wanted on his show. Our job was to make it happen and allow his genius to flower. He would come into the studio for the series, set up on Sunday nights, tape opens and closes to the show on Monday, and on Tuesday and Wednesday tape all thirteen programs back to back. We would preview them on Thursdays, and then on Fridays tour the countryside around Muncie looking for Albany Glass, a collecting hobby Bob had developed along with my wife.

To me, Bob was our superstar. He was fun to be around and to work with. He loved to laugh, play practical jokes, and often would surprise us with various twists in the routine of producing the shows. When I traveled and asked seatmates on my plane about their awareness of Bob Ross, inevitably they all had stories about how they or family members or friends watched and appreciated what Bob was doing on *The Joy of Painting*.

My favorite story is about the couple from a small town east of Muncie who had won a bid to purchase the painting Bob had painted on-air that night. They arrived late, after the painting had been completed, and came into the building at about 11:30 p.m. The place we held the auction had a number of stairs to get to the studio floor, and the woman was disabled, so she waited as we fetched the painting and Bob. When she saw him at the top of the stairs, she started to cry, and Bob quickly descended the steps and hugged her. What she said then has stuck with me to this day: "You're the best part of my day. Every day, I'm in constant pain, and I sit on the couch and watch you paint. When I'm watching you, the pain goes away. Thank you for making my time with you, the best part of every day."

As she turned and walked away, he cautioned her that the oil painting was still wet and they had to be careful to let it dry for a couple of weeks, and they smiled and said their goodbyes. As Bob and I walked up the stairs, I remarked to Bob, "What an amazing story. Have you ever heard that before?" And Bob said, "I hear that all the time. People think we're just painting, but I'm changing people's lives. That's why I paint. I love it."

What I know is that Bob is still changing people's lives. That night changed me and my understanding of what we were doing with Bob. And I know, beyond a doubt, why we were so successful with *The Joy of Painting*. As people watch the show, they are transformed from whatever they were into what they can become by buying into Bob's vision of happiness: focusing on what is good and happy and fortuitous in our lives, versus always looking for what is wrong and negative and frustrating. Bob always chose to see what was good, pure, and lovely, and to focus on what we can do—not what we wish we could have done.

At the end of every show, Bob chose to sign off by blessing each viewer with his parting gift: "Happy painting, and God bless." I thank God that Bob Ross walked into our station and asked, "Would you like to do a painting show?" because my life has been better ever since.

With rare exceptions, Bob's paintings put nature front and center—the ocean, a forest, a mountain.

Bob Ross
The Man

Inside the intensely private life of the painter with the
most famous perm on public television

"Back in the days when we used to listen to shows on radio—before TV was popular enough for my neighborhood to have one—I used to listen to some of the shows and they'd be sad at the end and I'd threaten my brother if he told anybody at school that I'd got sobby-eyed over some of these things."
—Bob Ross, 1990

The Early Years

by Gina McIntyre

Bob Ross was a medical records technician in the U.S. Air Force before he took up his first painting lesson at an Anchorage, Alaska USO club.

With his soothing, soft-spoken manner and his immediately recognizable mop of curls, Bob Ross wasn't the sort of flashy art world star likely to generate headlines. He wouldn't have a show at a trendy New York gallery or be anointed by critics as painting's Next Big Thing. Yet for millions of viewers, Bob Ross, through his long-running public television series, *The Joy of Painting*, fostered a critical appreciation of both the process of creating a work of art and the art itself. Ross made art accessible to the masses—he began each program with a blank canvas and concluded it with a completed painting. No matter your level of experience, if you followed along with Bob, you too could create a pleasing landscape to hang in your home.

On screen, Ross was a painter and a teacher. Behind the scenes, Ross was a savvy businessman who, with the help of his wife and friends, worked his way up from humble circumstances to become a much-beloved figure whose celebrity knew no borders. To many of his faithful viewers, Ross also came to feel like a friend, a reassuring, serene presence always happy to share his talents with the world. "He wasn't only a painter," says talk show host and superfan Phil Donahue, who once called Ross "the most famous painter in the universe." "He was an entertainer in his own right." Donahue went on to say, "Without any flash, his paintings spoke for him—he took you by the hand and led you along the way."

Off-screen, Ross was an intensely private man who zealously guarded details about his personal life. He granted very few interviews; much of what is known about Ross can be surmised from occasional remarks he would make as he was adding "happy little trees" to his paintings. Occasionally, he would allude to his loved ones or to significant events from his past—dreamy afternoons with his half-brother, his abiding love for his mother, a childhood fascination with nature. In the wake of Ross's death on July 4, 1995 at age 52 from lymphoma, those closest to him have continued to be respectful of the artist's privacy.

What is clear is that there was nothing about Bob Ross's early days that suggested

Above Bob (right) was best man at his brother Jim's wedding. "We used to fight like cats and dogs—you know how brothers are—he's a good man, though," Bob said of Jim in a 1993 interview. "He's my best friend in the whole world."

Opposite As children, Bob and Jim ran wild through the Florida woods. "And shoot, we were tough," Bob said. "We didn't even wear shoes back then. Don't think we had any."

he would become a television sensation and would amass a multimillion-dollar retail business selling how-to books, videos, and Bob Ross-branded art supplies. Born Robert Norman Ross on October 29, 1942, in Daytona Beach, Florida, the future entrepreneurial artist was the only son of carpenter Jack Ross and his waitress wife, Ollie. The family soon moved to Orlando, where young Bob, who enjoyed an especially strong bond with his mother, developed a passion for the outdoors that would influence his predilection for capturing the natural world on canvas.

"She had the largest influence on him," says Ross's longtime business partner Annette Kowalski. "She's the one who taught him the love of wildlife. Second to painting—or maybe even more than painting, Bob loved wildlife."

Said Ross: "Blender brushes are very, very soft. As my father used to say,

they're tender as a mother's love, and in my case, that was certainly true. I'm very prejudiced, but I think I had the greatest mother there was."

Ross's parents separated when Bob was very young, and his mother remarried briefly and had another son, Jim (Jack and Ollie would briefly reunite much later in Ross's life). The boys had little in the way of toys, so they turned to nature for amusement. "When I was a kid, I used to sit around, and my brother and I, we'd look at the clouds, and we'd pick out all kinds of shapes," Ross said. "We'd see the mean old witch or the candy man or whatever."

Young Bob had trouble at school, where he struggled as a student and earned generally poor marks. As he was painting on-camera, he once commented as he was offering instruction to the audience, "Do these little x's...see? Little x's...there. That's just the way the teacher used to grade my

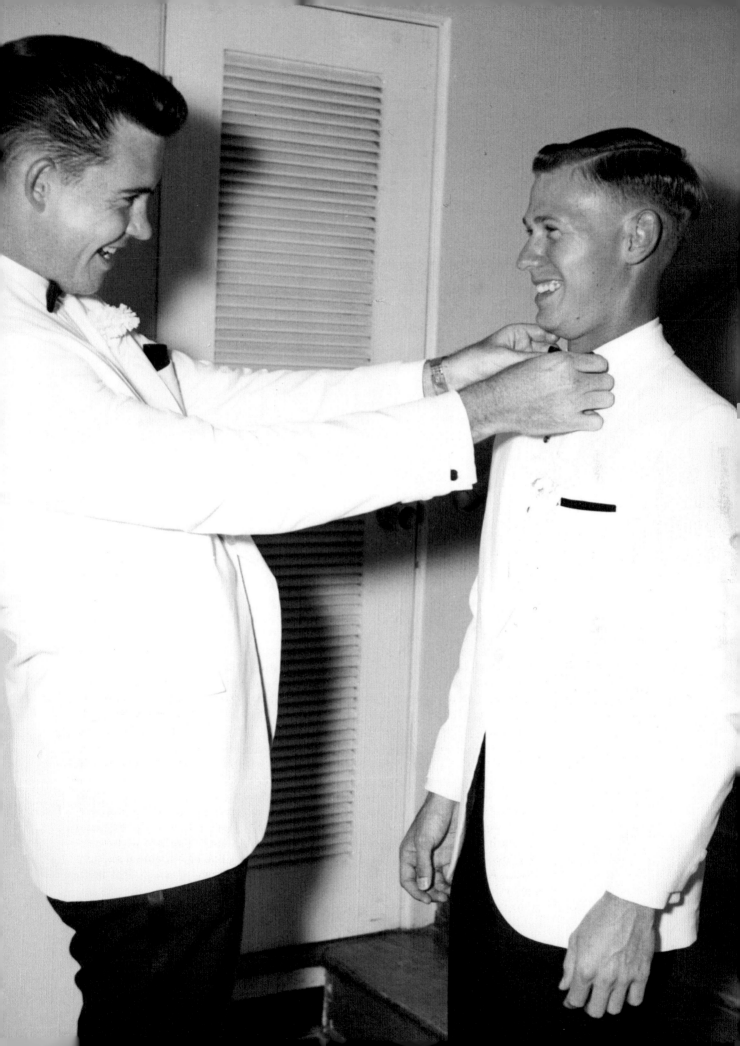

Above Bob didn't know how to fly, but he was a bit of a daredevil. He loved fast cars and had a vintage Corvette Stingray that he prized.

paper in school—she'd just run across it and go xxx..." But his academic struggles were no indication that he lacked curiosity about the world around him. Bob adored animals and often brought them home to care for them.

"I think when I was a kid I must have had every kind of pet imaginable," Ross said. "I lived in Florida, so I had access to a lot of creatures, but I had a pet snake. Man, he got out of the cage and was lost in the house for a long time. My mother got up and went to the bathroom one night—he was in there and scared her!" Adds Kowalski: "Bob says that they were not wealthy, and really, I think he viewed these wild animals— anything he could get his hands on—as toys and entertainment."

After Ross dropped out of school in the ninth grade, Jack Ross decided to teach his son carpentry to help enable him to earn a living. "I used to be a carpenter years ago," Ross said. "My father was a carpenter, and he taught me that trade. And I tell you what—it isn't that easy to make a shed or a barn." The lessons had an unforeseen consequence, however—he lost a finger during a woodworking project. "When there's a palette shot, you can see the missing finger," Kowalski says. "But because it was on his left hand and not his right hand, it didn't affect his ability to hold the brush."

Ross enlisted in the military in the early 1960s, joining the Air Force at age 18. Soon after, he married his first wife, with whom he had a son, Steve. Their union was short-lived, though, leaving Ross to raise Steve on his own in Florida for several years until the military transferred Bob to Alaska. "I had

been born and raised in Florida and was 21 years old before I ever saw snow," Ross said.

Ross quickly became accustomed to life in Alaska, remarrying and settling down near Fairbanks with his new wife, Jane, a civilian worker in the U.S. Air Force. For more than a decade, Ross served primarily as a medical records technician at the air base hospital, taking his first painting lesson at an Anchorage USO club. It was then that he discovered his love for oil painting and began to spend his free time putting images to canvas. "I spent half my life in the military, and I used to come home, take off my little soldier hat, and put on my painter's hat," Ross said.

He found inspiration in the snow-capped mountains that surrounded him—soon, he was selling his paintings to tourists. In addition to selling his landscapes, Ross found

yet another way to put his talent to use providing for his family. "He was a part-time bartender, and he was painting gold pans in Alaska and selling them in the bar to make money," Kowalski says.

It was while working in that Alaskan tavern that Ross would stumble across a television program that would radically change the trajectory of his life. One day, the tavern's set was tuned to a public television station broadcasting *The Magic of Oil Painting* hosted by German art instructor Bill Alexander. "About 1975, I saw Alexander on television, and like millions of other people, I fell in love with him," Ross said.

The thirty-minute program saw Alexander stand in front of a canvas, palette in hand, and speak directly to the audience as he completed a landscape painting. Alexander used the "wet-on-wet" technique,

Above Bob credits his mentor, Bill Alexander—host of the public television program, *The Magic of Oil Painting*— for teaching him the wet-on-wet painting technique. Bob referred to him as his "beloved friend and teacher. Bill taught me this fantastic technique, and I feel as though he gave me a precious gift."

applying layers of wet oil paint on top of one another to more easily blend colors. Ross left Alaska to study with Alexander in California, quickly becoming his star pupil. "I took one class, and I went crazy," Ross told the *New York Times* in 1991.

Although Ross's wife Jane remained behind in Alaska with Steve, she enthusiastically supported her husband's artistic pursuits. "She allowed Bob to leave Alaska with $1,000 and told him to either go out and make his fortune or come back home," Kowalski says. "He promised her, 'I'll go and do this. If it doesn't work, I'll come back home and do domestic stuff and be a good husband and father.' So, she stayed in Alaska and waited."

Below Bob's original easel was made from a converted stepladder. It has been acquired by the Smithsonian Institution.

OPENING A CLASSROOM

When Ross retired from the Air Force, he was offered a position with Alexander's Magic Art Company as a traveling art instructor. He taught classes across the country before landing an assignment in his home state of Florida. It was while he was teaching there that Kowalski decided to take a painting workshop; she and her husband Walt had recently suffered the loss of a child, and she hoped that learning to paint might help her work through her grief.

She enrolled in a five-day seminar in a hotel conference room in Clearwater, and became transfixed by Ross and his method of instruction. "I became aware of an effect that Bob was having on these students," Kowalski says. "Very calming effect, very quiet, I had never seen anything like it. I was mesmerized by him." Before returning to her home in northern Virginia, the Kowalskis invited Ross to dinner at a local hamburger joint and pitched the idea of launching their own series of painting seminars. He agreed, and the trio formed a new business partnership.

Still, finding students for classes offered in art stores and shopping malls initially proved difficult. "We would try to get Bob into a shopping mall and demonstrate, and in turn, try to recruit students for the classes that would occur maybe three days later," says Walter Kowalski. But, adds Annette, "We didn't have much success. Even though we ran expensive newspaper ads." At one point, they even created a toll-free hotline: 1-800-Bob-Ross. Although the going was slow, Ross himself was patient. "To me the first step in accomplishing anything is to believe that you can do it," he said. "Probably one of the most important things Bob said to me was, 'If you do what you love, the money will come,'" Kowalski says.

Still, with expenses mounting, Ross decided he could save money if he permed his naturally straight hair to avoid the need to pay for regular haircuts—a choice that would haunt him for the rest of his life. Once he became famous, the look became his signature. "He could never, ever, ever change his hair, and he was so mad about that," Kowalski says. "He got tired of that curly hair."

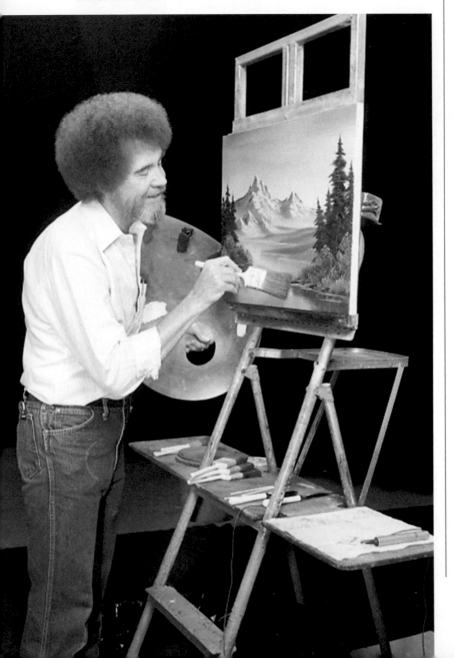

To help spread the word about Ross's painting seminars, Kowalski arranged for Ross to record a commercial with his retired mentor Alexander—the spot showed Alexander literally passing off his paintbrush to his former pupil. When the Kowalskis brought the clip of Bob painting to their local Virginia public television station, WNVC, the reaction they received astonished them. "When they saw Bob painting on this tape, they got very excited," Annette Kowalski says. "They came to us and said, 'Wow, this guy is wonderful! Would you agree to do a television series?' And we said, 'Would we ever!'"

The series, of course, was titled *The Joy of Painting with Bob Ross*. First broadcast in 1983, it became the top-rated show among art programs on public television, inspiring viewers to try their hand at creating works of art the same way Julia Child had helped her audience learn to love to cook. Yet even as the series' culture footprint began to expand and Ross's cultural star began to ascend, he remained as grounded as ever. Ross relocated back to Florida full time to live with Jane and Steve, and he was always happy to share his passion for painting with anyone who cared to tune in. "I have people in their nineties doing their very first painting," Ross told the *New York Times*. "I really believe that if you practice enough, you could paint the *Mona Lisa* with a two-inch brush."

Left Bob's first love was painting, but his affection for animals—particularly wild animals that needed rescuing—wasn't far behind.

BOB ROSS'S FAMILY

by Amy Wilkinson

The son of a carpenter and a waitress, Ross chose to keep his family in anonymity even as his star rose.

You know the permed-out Afro, the blue button-down shirt, and the gentle, hypnotic voice. But chances are, you know very little about Bob Ross's personal life. And that, by Ross's own admission, was by design.

"I stay hidden," Ross told the *Orlando Sentinel* back in 1990. "I'm sort of hard to find."

But once an outlet did find Ross, he claimed he was more than happy to chat. "I never turn down requests for interviews," he said. "I'm just rarely asked."

And that was the interesting nature of Ross's fame: *The Joy of Painting* had tens of millions of loyal viewers, yet the painter himself was hardly a blip on the celebrity world's radar. (Many publications, then and now, have compared Ross to his public television neighbor *Mister Rogers' Neighborhood*, and the comparison seems rather fitting.)

Yet, there are a few things we know about those who were close to Ross. The son of a carpenter (Jack) and a waitress (Ollie), Ross grew up in Florida, before enlisting in the Air Force and relocating to Alaska. In 1965, he married his first wife and the two had one child, a son named Steve, who would turn up on *The Joy of Painting* from time to time. He made his debut during the season 1 finale (introduced by his father as "the pride and joy of my life") to help with a question-and-answer session. With his tinted aviator glasses and blue button-down shirt, the younger Ross certainly looked the part!

Ross and his first wife divorced in 1977, and he later married his second wife, Jane. It was while married to Jane that Ross helped launch Bob Ross Inc., with former student Annette Kowalski and her husband, Walt. Jane died in 1993 from cancer just a couple of years before Bob died.

Today Ross's legacy is maintained and protected by the Kowalskis, who continue to run Bob Ross Inc. Though a private man until the end, he clearly had a fiercely loyal circle of friends and confidantes by his side.

Above Bob's mother Ollie was the love of his life. One of the highlights of her life was hiking and salmon fishing with Bob when he was stationed in Alaska.

This page Bob's wife Jane provided the stability a traveling artist and teacher needed living a hectic life. Jane cared for Bob's son, Steve, when he was little, and helped manage the business side of Bob Ross Inc. when it was formed in the early 1980s.

The Joy of Painting

by Gina McIntyre

It took years of hard work before his show achieved national success, but behind it all was a dedicated team of enthusiasts.

I t began with a simple greeting. "Hi. I'm Bob Ross, and for the next thirteen weeks, I'll be your host as we experience *The Joy of Painting*." That kindly welcome opened the first episode of Ross's landmark how-to series, which was designed to teach viewers that anyone, regardless of their background, could create original works of art. Ross's easygoing charm, his utter lack of pretense, and the intimacy he created with the viewer all marked the series as something special—a low-fi educational public television program with the potential for real lasting appeal.

The fact that interest in *The Joy of Painting*—and in its down-to-earth star—has only increased over the last few decades would no doubt surprise the humble Ross, a man from a modest background who simply wanted to share his passion for oil painting with the world. During his life, he worked tirelessly preaching the merits of artistic pursuits, a message that has now spread to a whole new generation of fans thanks to the series' widespread availability on streaming services and YouTube.

Yet, while there's no question that Ross prompted many people to try their hand at painting who otherwise might never have gone near a canvas, only 3 percent of his viewers were painting along with him at home. Rather, most tuned in to spend time with Ross himself. "The majority of our audience does not paint, has no desire to paint, will never paint," Ross told the *Orlando Sentinel* in a 1990 interview. "They watch it strictly for entertainment value or for relaxation. We've gotten letters from people who say they sleep better when the show is on."

But Ross never set out to become a television personality. In fact, his much-watched series might well be described as one of those "happy accidents" the artist would sometimes take note of while painting on camera. The show that became the centerpiece of a cultural empire was born largely because Ross was simply in the right place at the right time.

THE WNVC YEARS

After going into business together, Ross and his partners Annette and Walt Kowalski had

Above Bob does an interview with an Atlanta radio station in the early 1990s. Even though they couldn't see him, listeners tuned in to hear the sound of his brushes and his voice.

run into trouble. They were struggling to attract students to the classes that Ross was teaching in shopping malls and art stores—Ross just didn't have the name recognition to attract pupils. Hoping some advertising might turn things around, Ross taped a commercial with his mentor, Bill Alexander, the public television personality who had taught Ross to produce landscapes quickly using the trademark "wet-on-wet" technique.

The Kowalskis and Ross brought the spot to Falls Church, Virginia, PBS affiliate WNVC hoping to use the station's equipment to convert the commercial into a more widely used format. When the station executives saw the spot—with Ross painting a canvas in record speed—they were taken aback by Ross's talent and affable demeanor, and asked whether he might have any interest starring in his own television series. He did. The concept came together quickly, and *The Joy of Painting* officially debuted in 1982.

At the beginning of the show, Ross would start with a blank canvas and finish, less than thirty minutes later, with a completed oil painting. Every element of the show was thought out, from Bob's standard uniform of long-sleeve dress shirt and jeans to the soothing tone of his voice.

"He said, 'Annette, these television programs could go on for years'—little did he know—'I want to be sure and wear something on television that looks as good 30 years from now as it does now,'" Annette Kowalski says.

From the earliest days, Ross wanted to create a homey, comfortable space for viewers. Initially, he envisioned a log cabin-style setting, though Ross ultimately opted instead to place his easel in front of a simple black curtain backdrop. "Bob's original idea was to have this elaborate set," Walt Kowalski says. "It looked like a trapper's log cabin, but it finally dawned on Bob that he would not create the intimacy with the viewer with all of that in the background."

Ross took great pains to prepare before filming an episode. He'd begin by producing one finished version of the landscape that

Above Bob films a pro-motional spot for MTV. It was a bit of foreshadow-ing. Twenty-five years later, Bob would become an icon to Gen XYZ-ers.

he'd be painting on camera; although the audience never saw that original reference painting, Ross would occasionally look to it as he was re-creating the image on screen. "Bob insisted that nobody ever see the finished painting because sometimes he didn't have time to do everything that was in that painting, and he would have to leave out a big tree or a bush or a boat," Annette Kowalski says.

With *The Joy of Painting* underway, Ross had the idea for a series of illustrated instructional manuals that could serve as a companion to the series, offering step-by-step directions to reproduce Ross's paintings at home. But WVNC didn't have the means to pay for a book, leaving the Kowalskis to finance the project. "It was going to cost $30,000," Annette Kowalski says. "So, Walt mortgaged our house, and we published Bob's first book."

"When we wrote the first book, neither of us knew one thing about writing a book or publishing a book," she continues. "Bob, after he filmed a painting in front of the cameras,

we would then go back home and he would repaint that painting. I would stand behind Bob with my Canon 35mm camera. He would make me take about 50 photographs the whole time he was painting. Those were the how-to photos that he wanted in that book."

Season one of *The Joy of Painting* aired on public television stations across the East Coast, but viewership was limited and, owing to the poor quality of the audio and video, those first thirteen episodes never aired again (the companion book, though, would plant the seeds for a thriving publishing business). Soon after, the WVNC partnership dissolved, leaving Ross to return to teaching full time, and he and the Kowalskis in search of a new public television home—which soon led them to WIPB in Muncie, Indiana.

"Our dream was to move this inland to the Midwest," Annette Kowalski says. "Walt was tracking where Bill Alexander's program was popular. Those were the cities that we wanted to hit with our classes. Phil Donahue was very big in those days, and he was coming out of Chicago. We wanted to run commercials on *The Phil Donahue Show.*"

WIPB IN MUNCIE

Muncie is a small college town about an hour outside of Indianapolis, home to Ball State University. Ross and the Kowalskis had pulled into town for some seminars in the area, and hoping to spread the word, they chose to visit the local public television station headquarters, housed in the historic Lucius L. and Sarah Rogers Ball home.

"I was sitting in my office, and I look out the window and this VW bus pulls in the driveway," says former WIPB program manager Larry Dyer. "This bushy haired man gets out and this lady with him, and they come walking up to the door. He says, 'Well, hi! My name's Bob Ross, and we're doing a demonstration and some classes at your mall down the street and wondering if you could give any publicity to us?' And I looked at our production manager, and I said, 'Have we got a deal for you!'"

Their timing couldn't have been better. At that point, Congress had just approved a measure allowing select public television stations to accept advertising to help raise additional revenue; WIPB was among those

stations. Dyer's team produced a commercial promoting Ross's painting classes and aired it before and after Bill Alexander's program—the ideal time slot. The Kowalskis also bought air time on *The Phil Donahue Show* hoping to draw pupils from the greater Chicago area.

Their plans paid off; the seminars were filled with students—too many students, in fact—prompting Ross to wonder whether the station might be the right place to produce future seasons of *The Joy of Painting.* "They usually had fifteen to twenty people," says Jim Needham, who served as WIPB station manager from 1976 to 1992. "That was what they shot for. All of a sudden, Bob walks in the door [asking] to talk to the person in charge. I went downstairs to see him, and I said, 'Can I help you?' He said, 'Yeah. We'd advertised to do our workshop here, and we've got a problem...We usually get 10 or 15, sometimes 20 people to respond to our ads. We've got 70, and it's kind of messed up our schedule. That's the problem. The problem is we've got too many people.'"

Needham invited Ross to lunch, where Ross told the station boss about his experiences producing the first season of *The Joy of Painting* back east, and how he

Below Bob did painting demonstrations on shopping channel QVC in the early 1990s. As soon as the paint kits sold out, his time was up. He never got past the clouds before getting hustled off stage.

Opposite Bob and Joan Kowalski—current president of Bob Ross Inc.—get ready for a taping of *The Joan Rivers Show* in New York City in the early 1990s. Bob wanted it to look like Joan was doing all of the heavy lifting and he got the easy end of the stick.

would like to find a new partner for future episodes. Although WIPB had only modest facilities, Needham knew that the station would be able to offer the higher production values that Ross and the Kowalskis were hoping for. Needham ran the numbers and determined that it would cost roughly $1,000 to produce a single episode; the artist and his business partners scraped together the funds and within months, they were back in Muncie, shooting new installments of the series.

"Part of the thing that made it magical was it was a very limited space," Needham says. "It was a living room. We covered over the fireplace at the back end of the room behind where Bob would be standing. We blocked off the windows and the door. The carpet was on the floor so we had some sound dampening. It was really an intimate place...In the wintertime, if Bob would be

there, we'd have to shut off the heat because otherwise the [radiator] pipes would clink. The only times we ever stopped the show is he'd say, 'The pipes are clinking. We've got to start over.' Then we'd say, 'Oops. Forgot to turn it off.'"

But season two wasn't without its challenges. "One night, somebody broke into Bob's motor home two days before we were to start taping, and they stole all thirteen of the reference paintings," Annette Kowalski says. "That was the most spontaneous series that Bob ever did."

Apart from that unexpected mishap, that season set the template for how every subsequent edition of *The Joy of Painting* would be filmed. "We actually did the season in a week," explains Needham. "Bob would show up, and he'd have thirteen canvases that he had perfected to the point where he could do them in 26 minutes and 47 seconds. That was the timetable that we had to meet for public television so everybody could do their underwriting announcements, their station ID, and then go onto the next program. We had to hit the time frame every time.

"Sunday was a setup day," Needham continues. "Monday, we would do the opens and closes. Usually on Tuesdays, we would do six or seven shows top to bottom. Wednesday we'd do the rest. Thursday, we'd preview all of them and look them over and make sure they were complete, and then we'd call it done, if you will, like he did."

Richard Collins ran the camera into which Bob spoke. "The show was generally shot straight through, live to tape," Collins says. "Occasionally, if there was a technical problem or something like that, they would go back and do an edit. But he was producing those paintings as you saw it on television." Adds Annette Kowalski: "He was very proud of that, that there was no trickery going on."

GOING NATIONAL

With the filming of the second thirteen episodes completed, Needham and his team along with Ross developed a plan to help the fledgling series reach as many markets across the country as possible. At first, thirty public television stations agreed to carry the show—the response was so overwhelmingly positive that others quickly followed suit, and by 1984, *The Joy of Painting* could be seen in most parts of the country. Thirty stations had become 50; 50 had become 75. Eventually, the series would be carried on more than 300 stations in the U.S. alone.

Ross and Annette Kowalski still spent most of their time on the road together teaching painting workshops, but with the business beginning to grow, Bob's wife, Jane, left behind their home in Alaska to work for the business alongside Walt Kowalski in the basement of the Kowalskis' Virginia home. "Jane was very much involved," says Annette Kowalski. "She did the secretarial work and the office work."

It was up to Jane and Walt to respond to the flood of letters that had begun pouring in—in some cases, it was fan mail; in others, it was requests for Ross's instructional manuals, which were promoted before

and after airings of the show. "We included announcements that solicited people to send in checks for a how-to book," Needham says. "They started off, I think, at $9.95. They would send the letters to us, and we sent them on to Walter Kowalski in Virginia. Sometimes we had 300 and 400 letters a day. People were writing in from all over the country."

The Kowalskis' daughter, Joan, who now serves as president of Bob Ross Inc., can still recall the dramatic change that took place in the family residence. "I was in college when they started this crazy thing and came home one day for Thanksgiving, and the house was just transformed," Joan Kowalski says. "It was no longer a home. It was like a warehouse and a shipping dock."

Every quarter, Ross would return to Muncie to tape a new season of *The Joy of Painting*. He even relocated to Indiana

Above Bob mugs for the camera during a *People* magazine interview in 1991.

in 1987, renting an apartment near the television studio with a lake out back that was stocked with fish, which Ross, ever the lover of animals, would feed daily. He sometimes would even feature animal friends as guests on the show—squirrels became his trademark. Bobette appeared in several episodes in the eighteenth season; there was also Peapod, a squirrel that lived with Ross for about two years until the artist released the animal back into the wild. "This was not something we were happy with, or encouraged, but we allowed him to do it because Bob was Bob," Needham says.

Over time, Ross grew quite close with members of the WIPB team. Often, he and Needham would go antiquing together

Below Fueling up for *The Joy of Painting* with a piece of pizza.

with Needham's wife, Linda, in tow. "[Bob] developed a passion for Albany glass, which is made north of Muncie about 30 miles or so," Needham explains. "We would go out to antique stores and look for them. His favorite ploy [was] he would walk into an antique store, and he'd come back to the front in about three minutes and he'd say, 'Well, there's three or four of them here. See if you can find them.' He would know right away. It reminded me of a museum curator who looks at a painting and...they would know everything about the painting. That was Bob. He knew."

The atmosphere on set was always jovial. "Bob had a wonderful sense of humor, and so our days were spent, more or less, telling jokes and goofing off," recalls Bill Bryant, a member of the production crew. "The Bob you see on the show is the Bob that we all knew even behind the scenes." Adds Needham: "He loved working with us, we loved working with him. We all loved him—and Annette, too. Between takes, he would sit down on the front steps when it was warm outside and drink iced tea and talk and tell stories. What an incredible person."

In 1987, Ross was invited by Hank Snow, who was then co-host of the Grand Ole Opry, to be a celebrity guest at the legendary country music venue in Nashville, Tennessee, and Needham accompanied Ross as his guest. He can still remember when Snow brought Ross up on stage: "When they introduced them, the crowd just went nuts," Needham says. "He went up there—he was nervous at first—and he cracked a joke. Everybody laughed, and he was on his way. It was just a really cool thing to walk in there and have all these country music stars come up to Bob and say, 'Oh you're my favorite! I watch you all the time, and I paint with you.'"

Ross realized that with demand for his classes increasing, he simply wouldn't be able to teach enough seminars to keep up with interest. So, he created a team of certified Bob Ross Instructors who could work with students in his stead teaching the wet-on-wet method. He also introduced his own line of paints and brushes, which established his brand in the commercial art world, and continued to publish his how-to books.

GROWING CELEBRITY

In 1989, with the arrival of his first hard-cover title, *The Best of the Joy of Painting*, written with Annette Kowalski, Ross achieved still another level of success, making promotional appearances on such network talk shows as *The Joan Rivers Show*. Rivers introduced Ross as "America's favorite art instructor," and when she asked Ross about the reasons for his popularity, he responded, "I think it's because magic really does happen in thirty minutes, and there's no editing to these shows. What happens really happens."

By the early 1990s, nearly 300 episodes of *The Joy of Painting* were on the air in the U.S. and Canada. But international interest began to grow with the show appearing in such countries as Mexico, Costa Rica, Colombia, the United Kingdom, the Netherlands, Germany, Switzerland, Austria, Turkey, Iran, South Korea, and Japan. By now, Ross was arguably one of the biggest stars in the history of public television, and the host of the most popular art show of all time.

Yet his behind-the-scenes operation remained surprisingly modest. "It's very funny," says Joan Kowalski. "You think that Bob would pull up in some big limousine, and he would jump out and the paparazzi would be clippering, clip, clip, clip. But in fact, we were dragging easels. We were just a bunch of country folk in the big city."

Below Bob peers from behind a television screen during a photo shoot for a 1991 *People* magazine article.

Television appearances continued—Ross was invited to teach hosts Regis Philbin and Kathie Lee Gifford how to paint on their morning talk show in 1992, and the following year, he filmed a pair of twenty-second promos for music network MTV; one of the spots concluded with Ross describing MTV as "the land of happy little trees." In 1994, he appeared on *The Phil Donahue Show* and invited five audience members to come to the stage to paint alongside him. "The audience was just totally into this," Donahue says. "And when you're twenty-nine years on the air, with an audience every day, you get pretty good at reading audiences. This audience, at the time that he did our show, was totally rapt."

HIS FINAL YEARS

Although Ross's career was at its pinnacle, his personal life was starting to come apart. In 1990, he had relocated from Muncie to Macclenny, Florida, near Jacksonville, to be near his mother, who had fallen ill. In 1992, he lost his wife Jane to cancer, and his own health was starting to fail owing to a recurrence of lymphoma. He'd received an original diagnosis long before *The Joy of Painting* began, and although the illness had been in remission for years, it returned as Bob neared fifty. Few knew about his history with the disease save for his closest friends.

By the end of 1994, it had become clear that Ross was too ill to travel back to Muncie to film new episodes of his series. He had produced 403 episodes over a 31-season run, which ended in 1994. "Bob was unable to complete series 32," says Annette Kowalski. "I think he prepared ten or twelve of the paintings and then he couldn't paint anymore and so we were never able to film or tape those programs—but we do still have those paintings."

To ensure that Ross's mission of teaching the masses to paint could carry on long after his passing, The Bob Ross Art Workshop & Gallery opened its doors in New Smyrna Beach, Florida. "Traditionally, art has been for the select few," Ross told the *Orlando Sentinel*. "We have been brainwashed to believe that Michelangelo had to pat you on the head at birth. Well, we show people that anybody can paint a picture

Bob and business partner Annette Kowalski pose for a picture in Mexico in the late 1980s. Mexico was the first country outside of the United States to embrace Bob through product distribution, teacher training, and *The Joy of Painting* on television.

that they're proud of. It may never hang in the Smithsonian, but it will certainly be something that they'll hang in their home and be proud of. And that's what it's all about."

On July 4, 1995, Bob Ross died of lymphoma at age fifty-two. "He really touched a lot of people and made a difference in their lives," Needham says. "I think the painting made a difference, but what he said made a difference. We're all looking for hope in life, even today, and will always be. I think he was selling hope as much as he was selling painting."

THE LEGEND LIVES ON

The Kowalskis, while grieving the loss of their close friend, had to make a decision about the future of the series, and the Bob Ross business. Although there were hundreds of instructors trained in Ross's methods, including Annette Kowalski herself, it simply did not feel right to have anyone else step in to host *The Joy of Painting*. "There was a lot of pressure on us right after we lost Bob to replace him with another painter, and we talked about it," Annette Kowalski says. "I think the smartest decision we ever made was *not* to replace Bob with anybody else. He just will live forever."

And he has. Just as Joan Kowalski took over Bob Ross Inc. from her retired parents, a new generation of audiences has come to enthusiastically embrace Ross and *The Joy of Painting* in the modern era. The live streaming platform Twitch hosted a nine-day marathon of the show in 2015, which helped spark the current Ross renaissance among a certain set of fans. The episodes also can be found on YouTube, where, for example, one 1993 episode titled "Island in the Wilderness" has garnered more than 27 million views.

Additionally, Ross's work has benefited from museum exposure. In 2019, the Franklin Park Arts Center in Purcellville, Virginia, gave Ross a solo show titled "Happy Accidents: An Exhibit of Original Bob Ross Paintings." Free and open to the public, the exhibition featured twenty-four works from *The Joy of Painting*. "Bob Ross...wanted to teach other people to paint," curator Elizabeth Bracey said in an interview with

CNN. "It was just never a priority to have an exhibit. But art's purpose is to evoke emotion and reaction. And there's a very emotional reaction that people have when you see the paintings in person...It's amazing to see the beauty and the wonder that he was able to create with this very fast and simple technique."

Meanwhile, The Bob Ross Experience, a museum that will include Ross's re-created studio, gallery space, and painting workshop, is planning to open their doors inside the L.L. Ball home in Muncie. What's more, some of Ross's paintings and a portion of his fan mail will shortly become part of the permanent collection of none other than the Smithsonian Institution. It's a testament to the impact Ross made on his viewers—the thousands who wrote to him to express their gratitude for the joy he brought to their lives—and to the contribution he made to the world.

"I try to get people to believe in themselves," Ross told the *Orlando Sentinel*. "I tell people, 'You can do this.' And they write back and say, 'You were right. I can do this. And now I believe I can do anything.' And that's where it starts. You have to believe in yourself."

Below Bob Ross-Certified Instructor Faye Fletcher (front right) poses with her students, showing off their paintings, after a class in Georgia. "People, especially beginners, love to paint waterfalls," Faye says. "They're easy and they are real flashy!"

BILL ALEXANDER

by Amy Wilkinson

Long before Bob Ross took the mantle of painting guru, there was his mentor: a German art teacher who instructed him.

From 1974 to 1982, a German immigrant named Bill Alexander produced *The Magic of Oil Painting* on public television. When Ross debuted *The Joy of Painting* in 1983, it was seen as a passing of the torch from mentor and teacher to student.

Born in 1915 in Berlin, Germany, where his family had fled from their East Prussia home to seek asylum during World War I, William (Bill) Alexander grew up in poverty. He took an early interest in art, however, perhaps inspired by an itinerant painter who would visit the local villages. Alexander first tried his hand at "professional" painting as an apprentice to a saddle maker and carriage upholsterer, adding the final flourishes—typically landscapes or flowers—to the buggies. Soon he too became an itinerant painter, traveling around the countryside of East Prussia, before enlisting in the army and being sent to the front lines of World War II. Alexander was eventually captured and became a prisoner of war in France, where he would endear himself to the officers by painting pictures of their family members. After the war, Alexander emigrated to Canada, and it was while living in Toronto that he began developing what he called the "Alexander Method," a wet-on-wet painting technique drawing heavily from a more than 500-year-old style called "alla prima" that allowed him to finish a piece in just minutes. He began teaching the technique and, one day in the 70s, took on a new student named Bob Ross.

Ross had first gotten a taste of the joy of painting at the USO club in Alaska, where he was stationed as a master sergeant in the Air Force. When he retired from the military, Ross discovered Alexander's TV show. He decided to study under the painter and was hired as a traveling salesman and tutor for the Alexander Magic Art Supplies Company. Ross eventually struck out on his own, helped found Bob Ross Inc., and hosted his own TV show. Yet, Ross was quick to credit Alexander during his *Joy of Painting* debut, saying: "I learned this technique from a wonderful man that I think all of us had enjoyed for many many years on TV, Bill Alexander. Bill taught me this many years ago and it's just the most fantastic way to paint that you've ever seen."

Despite the kind words, as Ross's popularity grew, the two became estranged. Alexander would go on to publish a series of books on his technique before dying in 1997 at the age of 81.

This page Bill Alexander, host of *The Magic of Oil Painting,* put the joy of painting back into Bob's life. "For so many years, painting had got to where it wasn't fun anymore," Bob said in 1984. "It became work, until I had the opportunity to study with Bill and learn this fantastic technique, and he made it fun again for me. "

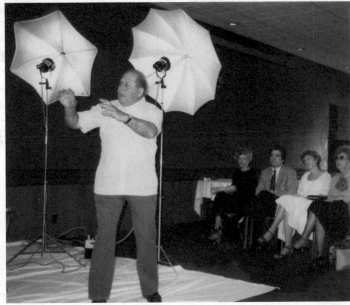

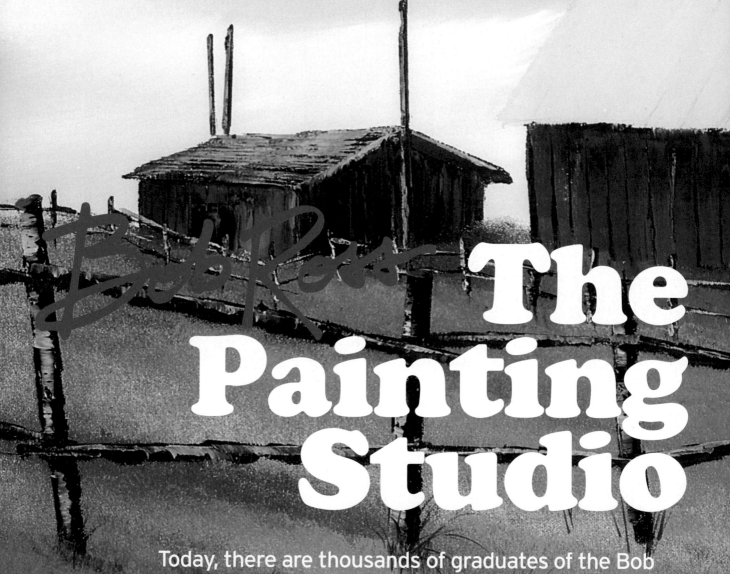

The Painting Studio

Today, there are thousands of graduates of the Bob Ross Teacher Training program across the world. But millions are seeking out *The Joy of Painting* videos with no intention of learning how to paint.

With the exception prepping a canvas with a layer of white paint, Bob did all of his famous show paintings in the thirty minutes of *The Joy of Painting*.

"There are no great mysteries to painting," Bob says in his instruction books. "You need only the desire, a few basic techniques, and a little practice." Once a pursuit that was considered for serious artists only, Bob made painting for everyone.

"Happy Little Accidents"

by Nancy Lambert

More important than the paint, the tools, or the technique, it's Bob Ross's gentle, encouraging style of teaching in *The Joy of Painting* that endeared him to generations of amateur artists around the world. Decades later, his instructors are carrying on both his method and his uplifting message: Everyone can paint!

In *The Joy of Painting*'s thirty-one seasons, one thing never changes: Bob Ross's unwavering belief that You. Can. Do. This. Too! His warm, inviting vibe wasn't accidental; it was a choice.

"Traditionally, art has been for the select few," Ross told the *Orlando Sentinel* in a 1990 article about the soaring popularity of *The Joy of Painting*. "We show people that anybody can paint a picture that they're proud of."

"It's that message that everyone could do what he was doing that really made Bob Ross," said NPR journalist Kat Lonsdorf in a recent *All Things Considered* segment, "The World of Bob Ross." She added, "Bob Ross told you that as long as you tried, it would be right, no matter what."

The idea that art is for everyone lives at the core of the Ross method—and the company he helped found in the early 1980s, Bob Ross Inc., still delivers that message to aspiring artists everywhere through a network of dedicated Certified Ross Instructors (CRIs®).

Today, decades after Ross's passing, there are more than 3,000 CRIs in the United States and Canada—all 50 U.S. states claim at least one—and nearly 1,300 CRIs in 36 countries around the globe, including Japan, Australia, Iceland, Mexico, and even Tobago, a remote Caribbean Island.

CRIs come from a multitude of backgrounds: recent high school graduates, retirees, stay-at-home parents, military veterans, and even Hollywood actors. For instance, David Arquette, known for the *Scream* film franchise, is also a Certified Ross Instructor and teaches classes in Los Angeles to raise money for local charities. "I love keeping [Ross's] dream alive," Arquette said in a recent *Spectrum News* segment.

Dedication to Ross's "dream" is pretty much a requirement for any aspiring CRI, because certification is a serious commitment, in both time and money. For certification in any one of the Ross verticals—Landscapes, Floral, and Wildlife—instructors must attend and complete three separate five-day seminars (Levels I, II, and III) at the Bob Ross Art Workshop & Gallery in New Smyrna Beach, Florida.

Each seminar focuses on developing the instructors' skills across three key categories: artistic skills (such as wet-on-wet painting techniques and learning about the various tools), teaching skills (like how to motivate beginners and correct student mistakes), and

Above A blind student paints with the help of his mother at a 100-person painting class at the Cincinnati Reds baseball stadium in 2017.

business skills (everything from class setup to promotion).

According to the promotional materials, the benefits of certification include the right to teach under the Bob Ross name, the promotional support of Bob Ross Inc.'s publicity campaigns, and connection "to the only truly growing activity in the art industry." But CRIs have discovered value beyond the benefits listed in the brochure, including confidence, community building, and self-discovery.

THE BOB ROSS METHOD

Bob Ross's unshakable faith in his viewers' ability to paint is at the core of his method and his teaching style—the belief that art is for all is one he shared again and again, on air and in interviews. He instilled confidence in his fans and students, which applied to their painting, but also extended beyond the easel.

"Bob's ability to captivate those watching into believing that anything is possible with a little practice, encourages many people to pursue their dreams, even if it's not painting," says CRI Jeremy Rogers, who started watching Bob Ross on YouTube while he was a junior in high school. "I really liked drawing, but I had never even considered painting," he says. "Watching Bob gave me a lot of hope that it was easy enough to try."

Rogers did try painting and enjoyed it so much that he kept going, practicing Ross's techniques until he improved enough to be accepted into his school's Advanced Placement art course. His portfolio—filled with Ross-technique paintings—received a perfect score. After graduation, Rogers turned his passion for painting into a career track, when he started the Ross instructor certification program.

CRI Faye Fletcher also discovered a confidence she never expected to find through Bob Ross. "Bob made me a thousand times more confident," says Fletcher, whose eighteen-year career as a CRI began with a Bob Ross Master Kit and a couple of canvases purchased at her local art store. "I literally went from a shy mom of three who thought she had no skills," Fletcher says, "to becoming a businesswoman with a large following of students."

Having found confidence through painting with the Ross method, Faye tries to nurture that same feeling in her students. "Representing Bob helps me remember that I should retain that patient and encouraging attitude that so encouraged me in the first place," she says.

That patience and encouragement is part of the reason Bob Ross was—and remains—so popular with amateur painters. "Bob was a genius when it came to teaching beginners," says CRI Eddie Cuervo, who discovered firsthand "how much Bob Ross inspired people" when he began assisting his husband, CRI Doug Hallgren, at the Bob Ross Workshop in 2007. (Hallgren was hired to manage the workshop, but has since been promoted to the corporate side, as Bob Ross Distribution's new product specialist and specifications analyst.)

"I had no background in art," Cuervo says, "never sat in front of a canvas to paint." But Cuervo was motivated to get certified. "I took the three-week seminar in landscape, florals, and wildlife. I actually started to get really good at it." Now, as a CRI, he's paying that forward. "You never know what talent is hidden in you until you actually try it," he says.

"Gaining confidence with Bob's technique comes from repetition and experiencing the feel of creating various elements of a painting with the knowledge

Above Future painting teachers take a three-week training course at the Bob Ross Art Workshop & Gallery in New Smyrna Beach, Florida, to earn their CRI (Certified Ross Instructor) status.

that they did not appear on your canvas by accident," says Nic Hankins, a long-time CRI and recently appointed Bob Ross Certified Teacher Trainer and Manager at the Bob Ross Art Workshop & Gallery. "The technique alone is marvelous," Hankins says, "but combined with Bob's unassuming presentation and reassuring words, it's impossible to feel like you can't paint."

It's important for CRIs to bring Bob's positive, supportive attitude to their instruction. "In the classroom, to a student, the CRI is Bob," says Hankins. "It becomes our responsibility to instill the same brand of confidence and comfort that Bob provided his viewers."

This is a responsibility that CRI Ted Simpson took to heart in his teaching style. "I wanted to show people that they too can do this!" Simpson says. Growing up, he was inspired to try "all kinds of art" after watching Bob Ross, but he didn't pursue certification until his wife gave him a Bob Ross Master Kit, rekindling Simpson's love of art.

"Becoming a CRI was the best decision I ever made," says Simpson. "I even lost 100 pounds to be in better shape so I could have the stamina to carry all the supplies around and stand for hours teaching!" Besides underscoring the commitment CRIs feel to their craft, Simpson's dedication points to some of the less-obvious ways Bob Ross's method inspires people to build new worlds for themselves off the canvas.

THE PAINTING COMMUNITY

On *The Joy of Painting*, Bob Ross spoke to the viewer directly and the relationship felt one-on-one. But through his Workshop, the CRIs, and his fans and students, Ross fostered a deep sense of community, one that is still expanding in ways Ross may not have imagined, but would certainly enjoy.

"I think that I was drawn to Bob for the painting, but I stayed because of the kindness," says Faye Fletcher, who found teaching provided just as many benefits outside the classroom as within.

"Probably my greatest rewards [are] the friends I've been blessed to make on this journey," Fletcher says. "I have students that have become more like family

to me than my own family. I show that kindness to my students and in return, those are the people that stick with me through the years."

Nic Hankins was also moved by the sense of community art inspires. "It was through Bob that I had my first exposure to the power of painting as a movement," Hankins says, "a way to share joy, enthusiasm, and gratitude for life with others."

Jeremy Rogers saw a common thread in his classroom. "I have a lot of fun engaging with the students," he says, "because most people interested in Bob's style of art are fun people!"

Some CRIs are taking that one step further, using Bob Ross's method to build

new communities and bonds where they are needed most. When he was struggling, U.S. Air Force Staff Sergeant Robert Kingery found comfort through Bob Ross, who also happens to be a fellow Air Force veteran. "I was having personal issues and in a dark place," Kingery, a recent CRI, explains. He recalled Bob Ross on public television from his childhood and sought him out online. "I started to play the Bob Ross YouTube channel at work and I started to feel a change."

"[Ross's] ability to soothe and calm is amazing," Kingery says. "From the moment he appears on screen you get this sense of calm that resonates into you and just makes you happy." Soon, Kingery's wife and his

colleagues also noticed the shift. "I became known as the Bob Ross guy at work," he says. That year, Kingery's wife surprised him with a CRI-taught painting class for his birthday.

"She saw a physical change in me—how happy I was painting and how happy I was helping my friends as we were taking the class." With her encouragement, SSgt Kingery explored becoming an instructor himself. "I was blown away at how happy I was learning the Bob Ross technique."

But he didn't stop there. Having found a path to healing for himself, Kingery wanted to share that with other veterans, especially those living with post traumatic stress disorder (PTSD). After he became

Certified Ross Instructors teach painting classes at community centers, art stores, churches, libraries, and homes. Class sizes have ranged from a single student to 300 aspiring artists.

a CRI, Kingery started teaching classes to fellow veterans.

"There is something soothing about the class," Kingery says, discussing the particular appeal of teaching the Bob Ross method to military veterans. "The ability to let go of your problems for a little bit of time and have the power to move mountains in your own little world."

He found that painting also gave his students a renewed sense of agency. "The power to be able to be in control for a little while is huge," Kingery says. "That feeling of hopelessness, powerlessness, and nothing going right goes away during the time you are painting."

But he's careful to keep the class flexible so that everyone is able to enjoy it, wherever they are that day emotionally. "The veterans can either engage in the class," he says, "or they can just chill, absorb what is being taught, and enjoy the moment of control."

"Being a CRI has changed my life,"

"I THINK THAT I WAS DRAWN TO BOB FOR THE PAINTING, BUT I STAYED BECAUSE OF THE KINDNESS." –FAYE FLETCHER

Kingery says. Now that he knows he has the ability to help others through painting, the way Ross helped him, Kingery hopes to continue teaching. "I plan to continue to teach classes while on active duty," he says, "and when I retire I plan to make it a full-time experience."

KEEPING IT POSITIVE

Of course, being a CRI comes with its own set of inherent challenges. But in the same upbeat fashion that Ross famously faced his "mistakes" in painting, his CRIs confront any difficulties that arise with a positive attitude.

For Ted Simpson, the business side of being a CRI spurred him to venture out of his comfort zone. "The biggest challenge being a CRI for me is cold calling locations," Simpson says. "Trying to get a new venue is similar to deciding to paint in the first place. You have to gather your courage and just try. Put yourself out there."

Similarly, Jeremy Rogers found keeping classes full required a different kind of

creativity. "I've had to think outside the box to find new ways to teach," he says. "I just pitched an idea to the parks and recreation department in my area, called 'Let's Paint in the Park!' and they loved it!"

"My biggest challenge is not going overtime in class," says Faye Fletcher, but she promises (with a laugh) that she's working on it.

Eddie Cuervo found the rewards and challenges of teaching were linked hand in hand. "The biggest challenge being a CRI is teaching someone who has no experience with painting," says Cuervo, "and the biggest reward is seeing that person with no experience learn how to paint."

SSgt Robert Kingery had a similar take. "I have had several students tell me before the class that they can't paint or they don't know how to paint," he says. But with Kingery's reassurance and encouragement, "by the end of the class those students walk out with a painting that they are proud of and a confidence that they were able to tackle something that they did not think they would be able to do."

Nic Hankins agrees. "It's remarkable to watch a student who began a course with trepidations create a beautiful painting," he says. "It's a transformation I never tire of watching!"

Though they all took unique journeys to becoming a CRI, there's one thing Ross's instructors seem to have in common: they love what they do. "Once I started teaching I found that spreading the joy of painting also made me happy," says Jeremy Rogers. Nic Hankins adds, "From the time I learned the CRI program existed, the die had been cast...I'd found my life's passion."

Maybe that's why CRI numbers grew 900 percent in the last two decades. "Any time you learn, you gain," Ross said. For CRIs this is certainly true—they all started out as amateurs, but by taking that first leap toward learning the Ross method, they gained new confidence, a better understanding of themselves and a joyful, compassionate community that shares their love of art. Now, it's up to the CRIs to encourage others— with Bob Ross's distinctive kindness and enthusiasm—to pick up a brush and paint new worlds of their own.

Certified Ross Instructor Doug Hallgren helped students Connie Boynton and Stacey Corletto learn to paint a beautiful beach.

Bernie Oropallo teaches a Bob Ross-style painting class at Art Basel Miami—a world-renowned international art fair staged annually in Miami, Hong Kong, and Basel, Switzerland—in 2016.

BECOMING A CERTIFIED ROSS INSTRUCTOR

by Amy Wilkinson

Though *The Joy of Painting* concluded filming in 1994, Bob Ross's trademark wet-on-wet technique continues to flourish thanks to the Bob Ross Teacher Training Program.

Much as it had been for his mentor Bill Alexander's company, Ross's dream was to have a roving band of painting tutors traversing the U.S. promoting his method. He shared his vision during the third episode of *The Joy of Painting* in 1983, prompting viewers to write in for more information: "One of the things that we're trying to do as we travel around and teach this almighty method is we're trying to gather up an army of teachers and soon we'll have teachers that travel this entire beautiful country teaching this fantastic method of painting."

Of course, the notion of itinerant instructors has largely fallen out of vogue, but there are plenty of Certified Ross Instructors around the globe carrying on his legacy. How does one become a Certified Ross Instructor? All you need is the desire to paint, the proper tools, and about $1,200.

Classes take place in person at the Bob Ross Art Workshop & Gallery in New Smyrna Beach, Florida. There are currently three different tracts to choose from: Landscape Instructor (CRI®), Floral Instructor (CRFI®), and Wildlife Instructor (CRWI®). Each has three different levels that must be completed in order to receive certification. All sessions are five days long and cost $395. No prior painting or teaching experience is necessary to register. The website promises that you will "learn to paint, teach, and promote yourself in the spirit of TV's Number One Art Show *The Joy of Painting*."

For those who want to experience a Bob Ross-style class but don't necessarily want to go through the rigors of getting certified to teach, you can take a Level I course at the Workshop and earn a certificate of attendance, or you can enroll in a class in your own city under one of the 1,500 fully accredited Bob Ross Certified Instructors in the United States.

As Ross would say: "All you need to paint is a few tools, a little instruction, and a vision in your mind."

Bob really did love trees. A 2014 analysis found that 91 percent of his paintings contained at least one tree.

Step-By-Step with Bob Ross

In just thirty minutes on his television show, Bob Ross would take you through the easy steps needed to create your own creation—just like this painting of *Under Pastel Skies*. Now, you too can create a scene of serenity with these easy instructions.

Materials

- 2" Brushes
- #6 Fan Brush
- #2 Script Liner Brush
- Large Knife
- Liquid White
- Indian Yellow
- Yellow Ochre

- Alizarin Crimson
- Phthalo Blue
- Midnight Black
- Titanium White
- Prussian Blue
- Van Dyke Brown
- Sap Green

- Dark Sienna
- Cadmium Yellow
- Bright Red
- Canvas Preparation

Use a 2" brush to cover the entire canvas with a thin, even coat of Liquid White. Do NOT allow the Liquid White to dry before proceeding.

Sky

Load a clean, dry 2" brush with Indian Yellow and working outward from the center of the horizon, use criss-cross strokes to begin painting the golden glow in the sky. Without cleaning the brush, reload it with Yellow Ochre and working upward blend this color into the sky area. Still without cleaning the brush, reload it with Alizarin Crimson and add this color to the sky, above the Yellow Ochre. Softly blend with horizontal strokes.

Load a clean, dry 2" brush with a small amount of Phthalo Blue and use criss-cross strokes to add this color to the uppermost portion of the sky. With Phthalo Blue still on the brush, tap in the basic shapes of clouds in the sky. Use a clean, dry 2" brush to blend the entire sky area with long, horizontal strokes.

Underpaint the water on the lower portion of the canvas with Phthalo Blue on the 2" brush; starting at the bottom of the canvas and working up toward the horizon, use horizontal strokes, pulling from the outside edges of the canvas in toward the center.

Mountains

The small mountain in the background is made with the knife and a mixture of Phthalo Blue, Midnight Black, and Titanium White. With firm pressure, shape just the top edge of the mountain. When you are satisfied with the basic shape of the mountain top, use the knife to remove any excess paint.

Then, with the 2" brush, blend the paint down to the base of the mountain. Load a clean, dry 2" brush with a very small amount of Titanium White and tap to diffuse the base, then gently lift upward to create the illusion of mist.

Moving forward in the painting, add a second mountain range with a mixture of Prussian Blue, Midnight Black, Alizarin Crimson, and Van Dyke Brown on the knife. Use the 2" brush to blend the paint down to the base of the mountain. Highlight the mountain with Titanium White. Starting at the top, glide the knife down the right side of each peak, using so little pressure that the paint "breaks."

Use a mixture of Phthalo Blue, Titanium White, and a small amount of Midnight Black for the shadow sides of the mountain peaks. Use the mountain-shadow mixture on the fan brush to indicate the foothills at the base of the second mountain range. Hold the brush horizontally and just tap downward.

Add the large mountain with a mixture of Prussian Blue, Midnight Black, Alizarin Crimson, and Van Dyke Brown on the knife. With the 2" brush, blend the paint down to the base of the mountain.

Highlight the large mountain with a small roll of Titanium White on the knife. Use the mountain-shadow mixture for the shadowed sides of the peaks. Tap to diffuse the base of the mountain, then lightly brush upward to create the illusion of mist.

Use the same shadow mixture on the brush to indicate foothills at the base. Use the darker mountain mixture on the 2" brush to extend foothills out from the base. Pull the color straight down into the water for reflections. Brush lightly across. Use Liquid White and a very small amount of Alizarin Crimson on the knife to cut in water lines and ripples.

3

6

7

Evergreens

To paint the evergreens, use the fan brush with the dark mountain mixture and Sap Green. Load the brush full of paint to a chiseled edge. Start each evergreen by holding the brush vertically and touch the canvas to make the center of the tree. Now, turn the brush horizontally and use just the corner to begin the process of making the branches. As you work down the tree, use more pressure, forcing the bristles to bend downward.

Use the 2" brush to extend the paint from the base of the evergreen trees to underpaint the foreground land areas. You may add tree trunks to the evergreens with a mixture of Dark Sienna and Van Dyke Brown on the knife. Make a "marbled" mixture of this dark brown and Titanium White to touch in highlights to the trunks with the knife.

Very lightly touch highlights to the evergreen branches with a mixture of the dark foreground color and all the Yellows (including Cadmium Yellow), to make Green. (You may first touch your brush into a very small amount of Liquid White to help your highlights "stick.")

10

11

Foreground

The rocks and stones at the base of the evergreens are underpainted with a mixture of Dark Sienna and Van Dyke Brown on the knife. Use a "marbled" mixture of the same brown color and Titanium White on the knife and very little pressure to highlight the rocks.

Load a clean, dry 2" brush with the various mixtures of the dark evergreen color, all the Yellows, and a small amount of Titanium White and Bright Red to add the soft grassy highlights to the foreground. Hold the brush horizontally and gently tap downward. Work in layers, carefully creating the lay of the land. If you are also careful not to destroy all of the dark color already on the canvas, you can create grassy highlights that look almost like velvet.

Finishing Touches

Use the point of the knife to scratch in just the indication of small sticks and twigs. Enjoy your amazing masterpiece and don't forget to sign it with pride.

THE INSPIRING LANDSCAPES

by Amy Wilkinson

Ross's childhood in Florida and service in the U.S. Air Force in Alaska added color to all of his paintings.

All those "happy little trees" and "almighty mountains" featured in Bob Ross's idyllic paintings weren't just figments of his imagination—the artist drew upon a wealth of stunning real-life inspiration.

Born in the sunny coastal city of Daytona Beach, Florida, and raised in Orlando, Ross enlisted in the United States Air Force in his late teens and spent a portion of his twenty years of service stationed near Fairbanks, Alaska, living among the rugged crags and snowy climbs of the forty-ninth state. It was there, at the USO club in Anchorage, that Ross actually took his first painting class—and the surrounding cliffs would soon become his muse.

"When I was learning...I would cover a whole canvas with nothing but mountains and scrape it off and do it again," he would later say during an episode of his public television show *The Joy of Painting*. Nearby Denali (formerly known as Mount McKinley) seemed to be a particular touchstone for Ross: The second-ever episode of his series, which aired January 11, 1983, instructed viewers on how to paint the majestic peak. (Very few episodes were ever named after a real locale. Most were simply an idea—"Tranquil Wooded Stream," "Golden Glow of Morning.")

The Alaskan landscape also helped support Ross during his early years. To supplement his Air Force pay, he would paint scenes on novelty prospecting pans and sell them to tourists.

When he left the service, Ross returned home to Florida, and his coastal roots are also evident in his work (see: episodes like "Ocean Sunset" and "Windy Waves"), though they figure much less prominently. In fact, the blog FiveThirtyEight did a statistical

Bob was inspired by scenes from nature, such as this sunset on a river in Pennsylania, an Alpine lake in Switzerland, or the Alaskan wilderness.

analysis of subject matter of the 381 paintings Ross completed during his television series and discovered 91 percent had at least one tree and 39 percent had at least one mountain, while only 9 percent featured waves and 7 percent featured a beach. The mountains, he once told the *Orlando Sentinel*, were "the most popular pictures. We get letters every day from people wanting more mountains. As many as I paint, they still say, 'Give me more mountains.'"

Yet, whether he painted a snowy sunset or a balmy beachfront, all of Ross's myriad landscapes shared one thing in common; virtually no people.

"I can think of two times he painted people," Annette Kowalski, co-founder of Bob Ross Inc., told FiveThirtyEight. "There was a man by a campfire, and two people walking through the woods. If you notice, his cabins never had chimneys on them. That's because chimneys represented people, and he didn't want any sign of a person in his paintings."

And so, perhaps all those little trees of Ross's were so happy because they suffered no interference from man.

Godfather of ASMR

by Colleen Bordeaux

It turns out that Bob Ross's voice does more than give helpful instructions on painting: it also triggers an autonomous sensory meridian response in most people.

Two decades after his death, Bob Ross became a YouTube sensation. The grainy 1980s episodes of *The Joy of Painting* racked up view counts in the hundreds of millions, and amassed nearly 4 million followers—many of whom had little or no interest in picking up a paintbrush. His viewers sought out Bob Ross because they enjoy listening to his slow, soft voice and the calming rasp of his painter's tools against the canvas.

And they aren't alone. Bob's voice elicits a euphoric sensory experience that is today known as ASMR, or autonomous sensory meridian response, in millions of people.

The sensation—a tingling that starts in the scalp, trickles down the spine, and eventually relaxes the whole body—is a buzzy term in health and wellness. But it's highly subjective and hard to document, which are reasons why the phenomenon has not attracted much attention in the scientific community despite the millions of people who claim to have experienced it—and who flock en masse to videos of people folding towels and scratching microphones.

Bob Ross's voice is one point of consensus among the largely anecdotal and self-reported data. He's the classic example of an ASMR trigger, according to Craig Richard, a Shenandoah University physiology professor who has been researching the phenomenon.

Ross's baritone voice "just turned my brain to fuzz," says Richard, recalling his childhood viewing habits. "I didn't watch it to learn to paint. It was a way to relax and fall asleep after school." Richard gave little thought to the relaxing effect Bob Ross's show had on him until the summer of 2013, when he listened to an episode of the *Stuff Mom Never Told You* podcast. In it, they discussed how some people experienced pleasurable "brain tingles" while watching certain videos, or hearing certain sounds.

"I connected with exactly what they were talking about, realizing that I had experienced it [myself]," says Richard. He learned from the podcast that the brain tingle phenomenon was called autonomous sensory meridian response. Richard began searching for more information on the topic, and quickly discovered very little actual scientific research into the anomaly existed.

THE SCIENCE BEHIND ASMR

In 2010 ASMR received its official name, and it did not come from the scientific community. Jennifer Allen, a woman who had experienced the sensation while watching a video about the galaxy, spent

Viewers tune in to *The Joy of Painting* not only to learn how to paint but for the sense of relaxation brought on by Bob's soothing delivery.

years trying to quantify the effect. During her search, Allen found others in online forums who described the common phenomenon as a brain orgasm, but she felt more clinical language was warranted to legitimize the experience.

So she made one up, telling the *New York Times* in 2019 that she selected "autonomous" because it referenced an internal, spontaneous feeling; "sensory" because it was a sensation; "meridian" to suggest pleasure and give a nod to traditional Chinese medicine energy pathways; and "response" indicating that it happened as a reaction to external stimuli (like watching Bob Ross softly applying brushstrokes to a canvas).

There are countless videos and sounds that induce ASMR, but Bob Ross is regularly discussed when describing the phenomenon. He's considered the Godfather of ASMR because he embodies the core principles of ASMR triggers: "a gentle voice, soft movements, and helpfulness," says Richard.

something to relax you, and you're a passive recipient of their actions."

During guided meditation, practitioners receive instructions to achieve a relaxed state, so the words and the script matter, he explains. "In ASMR, it doesn't matter what they say, as long as they're doing it in a soft voice," says Richard. "What ASMR is bringing to light is that it may be more important how you say it, how you act [instead of the words you use]."

THE BENEFITS OF ASMR

Once inspired to dig into the science behind the phenomenon, Richard founded ASMRuniversity.com. His collaboration on a number of research projects included Allen as well as Karissa Burnett, a PhD candidate in clinical psychology at the Fuller Graduate School of Psychology in Pasadena, California, as the three seek to establish a fact-based foundation of knowledge about the topic. Their studies include determining what triggers ASMR, why it happens, who can experience it, and how it impacts those who experience it.

The group has collected data from more than 30,000 participants sourced through public ASMR community forums, such as Reddit. Roughly 66 percent of the study participants self-reported experiencing ASMR on one or more occasions, and provided additional information on benefits they received, including stress reduction and relief from anxiety and insomnia. To better understand the experience and benefits, the team has an ongoing survey collecting data.

Their survey is not alone. Other physiological and biological studies also appear to support the hypothesis that individuals who experience ASMR receive benefits from the phenomenon. For example, ASMR can lower your heart rate an average of 3.14 beats per minute, according to a study by The University of Sheffield. That study found ASMR to be a reliable, scientifically proven experience that may have therapeutic benefits for mental and physical health.

"Our studies show that ASMR videos do indeed have the relaxing effect anecdotally

> ## "DO YOU KNOW BOB ROSS? DOES HE RELAX YOU? YOU MAY HAVE EXPERIENCED ASMR," —CRAIG RICHARD

"Because he was so popular and widely watched, he is how many people make the connection [to ASMR]."

It's as simple as asking, "Do you know Bob Ross? Does he relax you? You may have experienced ASMR," says Richard. "Fred Rogers, or Mr. Rogers, is another example. He talked gently, softly, slowly in a caring way." This triggers the same type of sensation in the brains of his viewers.

The Bob Ross effect has also been associated with meditation, another new age practice. You can even hear Ross's voice in the Calm.com phone app, where he is a "narrator." The app helps listeners fall asleep and offers three audio files of Ross's voice under their "ASMR" category.

Although meditation and ASMR have similarities, Richard stresses that ASMR is a distinct phenomenon and should be viewed separately. "Meditation is a relaxing state that you put yourself into for the most part," says Richard. "ASMR is someone else doing reported by experiencers—but only in people who experience the feeling," wrote Dr. Giulia Poerio, a member of The University of Sheffield's Department of Psychology, on the university's website. "This was reflected in ASMR participants' self-reported feelings and objective reductions in their heart rates compared to non-ASMR participants. What's interesting is that the average reductions in heart rate experienced by our ASMR participants was comparable to other research findings on the physiological effects of stress-reduction techniques such as music and mindfulness."

According to a brain scan study conducted by Richard and his counterparts, ASMR activates similar regions of the brain that typically light up when someone receives "soothing social behavior" or positive personal attention, such as from a person calmly sitting close by or gently touching you. These findings line up with studies of what happens in primate brains when they are on the receiving end of grooming, says Richard. Since the most common triggers for ASMR are light touch and whispering, this makes logical sense.

"Think about how you comfort an infant," explains Richard. To sooth a child, parental figures often speak in a whispered or soft tone of voice and gently rub their back. The pattern repeats for all ages, says Richard. We instinctually sense "when it's more important to touch someone or hold someone's hand than to say something or do anything else."

The regions in the brain that are activated by these kinds of social bonding behaviors release dopamine, oxytocin, and endorphins. They increase empathy, social cognition, and caring feelings toward others. ASMR's activation of similar brain regions could associate the phenomenon with those same benefits, says Richard's study.

Simply put, the research suggests that the soothing, comforting effect people feel when they receive positive attention from a kind, caring person in the real world can be triggered through ASMR—and doesn't require physical touch to do so. Videos featuring soft voices and visuals of experiences ranging from moments with hairdressers to slowly opening boxes

can bestow the same benefits to some viewers as a hug.

While there is more work to be done to completely understand the clinical potential of ASMR, the foundational research has begun, says Richard. More than 50 percent of the participants in his data set that experience ASMR have self-reported that the phenomenon provides them relief from symptoms of depression, anxiety, and insomnia.

Relief from other conditions, such as PTSD, ADD, ADHD, and bipolar disorder, have also been reported through The Voices of ASMR survey. There are even cases of parents using ASMR to help their children cope with autism.

"My son has severe autism and extreme violent behaviors. Medication and ABA therapy only does so much for him. ASMR has made a huge difference in helping him be calm, less anxious, and fall asleep easier," said one respondent. Her comments were repeated by others, who remarked on how ASMR videos provided "a great soothing and relaxing environment for [my] children."

In another study conducted by the Department of Psychology at Swansea University in the United Kingdom, 70 percent of the participants reported using ASMR to reduce stress. An additional 42 percent of the participants reported reduction in chronic

The combination of Bob's lilting voice and the gentle sound of the brush strokes is what triggers the ASMR effect. Here, he paints *Gray Mountain*—a fan favorite because of the glowing sky—in 1991.

pain through several common triggers including crisp sounds and slow movements. The study also indicated temporary improvements in symptoms of depression.

Additional studies have echoed the findings. According to the Sheffield University study, the interpersonal nature of many of the triggers (e.g., whispering) suggests that ASMR may have an impact on social (as well as nonsocial) feelings. This could be a reason why the resurgence of interest in Bob Ross and ASMR is coinciding with the growing loneliness epidemic. In 2018 in a report by Cigna, more than half of Americans stated they often or sometimes feel lonely, and lack meaningful social interactions.

With millions of people craving positive, personal attention from a kind or caring person in the real world, it's not surprising people are gravitating toward virtual channels that replicate similar feelings through ASMR, such as Bob Ross episodes on YouTube.

Anecdotal experiences seem to support that as well. "Our life is isolating," wrote one respondent to Richard's study, whose son suffers from microcephaly. "I only have a few friends that I see every so often. When watching [ASMR] videos I found that these wonderful artists were also keeping [me] company."

INTENTIONAL USE

What's important to remember is that Bob Ross "wasn't trying to relax anyone, he was trying to teach them to paint," said Richard. It's a great example of how Bob Ross's voice, tapping brush, and scraping knife are unintentional ASMR triggers. Researching why and how Bob Ross and others unintentionally evoked ASMR in viewers has allowed the phenomenon to be intentionally implemented in video and audio forms.

Maria, a thirty-three-year-old Russian who prefers not to give out her last name, was one of the earliest people to purposefully create videos to trigger ASMR. She started her YouTube channel GentleWhispering in 2011, after using ASMR videos to help her with depression following a divorce in 2009. Today, her channel has over 2 million subscribers and she launched a cottage industry of other "ASMRtists" who create videos designed to deliver brain tingles to their viewers.

To date, there are more than 13 million videos on YouTube, and more than 10 million posts on Instagram using the hashtag #asmr, with content ranging from crinkling and chewing noises to simulated experiences with nurses, doctors, hairstylists, and masseuses. The more popular ASMRtists, like Maria, have made intentional ASMR a full-time job thanks to follower counts in the millions that help drive advertising and sponsorship revenue.

It's not just YouTube and Instagram influencers catching on. ASMR is also being used in creative marketing promotions to influence positive brand association. Richard has been working with companies, such as JetBlue and Anheuser-Busch, to help them understand what ASMR is and how to create triggers in advertisements. It's begun a shift in philosophy about how to reach consumers: when you think about how to create an advertisement that catches someone's attention, "traditionally, it's been about raising alert systems," says Richard, yet "research shows that people like to feel relaxed, they enjoy it when their brain calms down."

Instead of trying to shout the loudest to capture attention, ASMR-inspired advertising aims to relax the viewer. Brands attempt to catch the attention of the YouTube ASMR community by building content for the platform, and also by integrating ASMR triggers into more conventional forms of marketing.

For example, JetBlue created a 9-minute "AirSMR" video on its YouTube channel to help viewers achieve a relaxed state and reduce stress using airport sounds. In the video, a woman's voice slowly and calmly narrates an experience in the JetBlue terminal at JFK, filled with soft sounds of voices, footsteps, fingers tapping on a keyboard, and crinkling snack bags. Although the tactic generated press coverage with features in the *Washington Post* and MSN, the video on JetBlue's YouTube channel performed poorly, receiving just over 30,000 views since it aired in Dec. 2019.

Two years earlier, IKEA produced an ASMR advertisement to their YouTube viewers. It featured sounds of sheets rustling on a mattress, being scratched and tapped by a pair of slowly moving hands, all narrated by a calm voice explaining how to create the perfect dorm room. Called "Oddly IKEA," the video generated a flurry of media coverage, including BBC and *Adweek*, and has reached nearly 3 million views.

ASMR has even made it to the Super Bow. Anheuser-Busch's 2019 ad featured actress Zoë Kravitz whispering into a microphone, tapping her fingernails on a bottle, and slowly pouring beer into a glass in an attempt to draw the event's 100 million viewers into the commercial instead of the traditional bold, splashy segments competing for their attention. Although the spot received mixed reviews, it did get noticed, generating 750 tweets per minute and 4,200 brand mentions in the hours following its debut.

BuzzFeed, Zippo, and KFC are other examples of brands taking notice of the new frontier ASMR represents to marketers, providing the opportunity to think about the sensory experience consumers have with a product.

EXPERIENCE IT YOURSELF

Not everyone can experience ASMR, says Richard, adding that there are also people who simply cannot find an ASMR trigger through video—but can in person. It's easy

THERE ARE MORE THAN 13 MILLION VIDEOS ON YOUTUBE, AND MORE THAN 10 MILLION POSTS ON INSTAGRAM USING THE HASHTAG #ASMR

to test for yourself. "You need to do it the same way you approach a buffet of food: be patient, and sample widely," says Richard.

He recommends starting with YouTube videos or podcasts focused on the more common triggers, including light touch and whispering, and being patient as you explore—after all, there are literally millions of options to choose from.

One simple place to start exploring this phenomenon yourself is with the Godfather of ASMR himself: watch a few episodes of *The Joy of Painting* on Bob Ross's YouTube channel to see if he can turn your brain to fuzz, just like he's done for so many others.

Bob once predicted that his paintings would never hang in the Smithsonian. He was wrong.

Bob Ross
The Legacy

When Ross passed at the age of fifty-two, he could never have predicted how many people would mourn his passing or plan to visit his art in museums.

The first real Bob Ross original painting exhibit opened at the Franklin Park Art Center in Purcellville, Virginia, in 2019. All of the event passes were reserved within 10 minutes of availability.

Belongs in a Museum

by Colleen Bordeaux

Bob Ross's "art is for everyone" philosophy and authenticity is why his work resonates with viewers—and why museums like the Smithsonian welcome his paintings today.

"My paintings will never hang in the Smithsonian," Bob Ross told talk show host Phil Donahue in 1990. The critics in his heyday agreed, judging his art-is-for-everyone philosophy and thirty-minute landscapes as kitschy and unworthy of acclaim.

As it turns out, Bob Ross and his critics were both wrong. In 2019, the Smithsonian acquired several of Bob Ross's paintings and other objects that they plan to place on display, first in a new acquisitions exhibit at the National Museum of American History, and eventually as part of a larger, long-term exhibit.

The Smithsonian is not even the first museum to formally recognize the impact Bob Ross had on millions of Americans and people across the world. A slew of exhibits at museums began cropping up in 2019 to honor his legacy, acknowledging his enduring relevance and the growing resurgence of interest in his work.

Bob Ross considered himself a teacher, not an artist, and this distinction is one of the reasons why critics who had elitist views about art shunned his work, according to

Elizabeth Bracey, a museum curator. Bracey presented the first collection of Ross's work at the Franklin Park Performing and Visual Arts Center in Purcellville, Virginia, about forty miles from Washington. "[The criticism he received] was understandable and indicative of the way art is and has been for centuries," she said, noting that his critics focused on the art itself when Bob Ross's mission was about the process: "He did not promote himself as an artist," she said. "He wanted to be known as someone who inspired others to create art."

Bob Ross built a following by emphasizing the joy of the creative process, rather than the value of the output, and represented a shift in philosophy. Art was no longer pretentious or exclusive, but instead egalitarian and inclusive. He believed that "there is an artist deep down inside each one of us" as he liked to say to his students through the airwaves.

The millions of viewers who tuned in to his public television show on their grainy 80s television sets would listen to Bob emphasize his philosophy that every person has innate creativity that can be cultivated and developed. "The secret to doing anything is believing you can do it," he'd say, while explaining a traditional wet-on-wet painting technique in a simple, no-frills way that anyone would replicate in their living rooms.

He also used humor to inspire his viewers to approach their creative process with confidence and joy instead of fear about how it would be perceived. Ross would occasionally even poke fun at art critics themselves, saying things like, "They say everything looks better with odd numbers of things. But sometimes I put even numbers—just to upset the critics."

Ross's "art is for everyone" philosophy, combined with his authenticity and ability to strike a human connection through a screen, is why his work resonated with his viewers and continues to attract the attention of younger generations decades later, according to Bracey.

On top of his refreshing philosophy and ability to connect with people, experiencing a man with a fluffy perm speaking calmly while applying soft brushstrokes to a canvas was a form of escape for his viewers from a stressful, tumultuous world. It's the reason why so many people with no interest in painting watched his show in the 80s and 90s. It also drove a recent resurgence of interest in his work when more than 5.6 million people across the world tuned

in to a marathon of his episodes as part of the 2015 launch of the social video platform called Twitch Creative that enables musicians and artists to livestream their works in progress.

The museums exhibiting Bob Ross are focusing on his philosophy and the movement he created, the experience he represents to millions of people, and the impressive proliferation of paintings he created in thirty-minute segments in front of an audience.

THE FIRST EXHIBIT

More than 15,000 people from across the world came to the first Bob Ross exhibit in fall of 2019, tripling the small town's population for four weeks and blowing away the expectations of the community art museum where it was hosted. "We didn't know what we were getting ourselves into," says Bracey, who had casually offered her museum space to Joan Kowalski, the president of Bob Ross Inc. located in nearby Herndon, Virginia, during a local art advisory committee meeting.

It was the first authentically curated Bob Ross exhibit, says Bracey, so "it just blew up—we had requests from national, international news outlets wanting to do interviews," including the *Washington Post*, BBC, NPR, CNN, the *Today Show*,

Bob Ross exhibit visitors—including his business partner Annette Kowalski (below left, in red)—study his paintings up close at Franklin Park Arts Center in Purcelleville, Virginia.

and even a spot on a national South Korean television program. Bracey herself did more than fifty interviews about the exhibit.

Given the unanticipated popularity, managing the visitor experience became a priority. "People being crammed like sardines would be the opposite" of the calm, peaceful environment Bob Ross sought to create, says Bracey. The museum opted to use a limited quantity of timed entry tickets, which sold out within days.

"At least once per day, someone walked into the gallery and cried," says Bracey. "People came because they had a strong connection to the person [they got to know while] watching *The Joy of Painting*, and the creativity [he helped them find] within themselves."

The level of global interest in this small exhibit speaks to the enduring relevance of Bob Ross. "His demeanor, his calmness, his joyfulness" resonates in our divisive culture and difficult world, says Bracey.

His ability to reach out through the screen, strike a real human connection, and empower people to find the creativity within themselves transcends time and generation. The popularity of this first exhibit was driven by "the Bob Ross renaissance happening with younger audiences," says Bracey. "I didn't introduce my daughter to Bob Ross, she found him on her own," noting that it was her daughter's love of Bob Ross that prompted her to ask Kowalski about exhibiting his work.

In addition to the peaceful experience he created, Bob Ross was an excellent art teacher. The techniques he used were not new, but he "simplified the method, perfected the tools," and distilled the process into a repeatable model that anyone could do from their living room, says Bracey. If you follow his guidance, "you are going to leave with a really great painting. It's like a recipe."

THE MUNCIE STUDIO

The Joy of Painting was filmed and broadcast from public television station WIPB in Muncie, Indiana, about fifty miles northeast of Indianapolis and home to the famous Ball Brothers Glass Manufacturing Company (now Ball Corporation) and their namesake Ball State University.

WIPB was based in a historic home formerly owned by L.L. Ball, and the first permanent exhibit dedicated to Bob Ross was opened there in late 2020 in the very studio where he painted in front of television cameras. The connection to the Ball family is significant not just because they formerly owned the home where Bob Ross filmed, but also because they saved the WIPB station that Bob Ross used to reach millions of viewers.

"Ed Ball, a son of the Ball glass founder, was really critical in making sure public television survived and got off the ground nationally and locally helping to get our station [WIPB in Muncie] solid and moving," says Jessica Jenkins, director of collections at Minnestrisa, the museum that owns the house and who curates the $1.2 million permanent exhibit and painting workshop series that opened its doors in 2020.

The museum has owned the property for years and only recently realized it was the home of *The Joy of Painting* back

Below A free 300-person painting class at TwitchCon 2017 in San Diego, California.

in the 1980s, says Jenkins. Once they discovered the connection to the famous painter, the museum contacted Bob Ross Inc. to re-create the space into a public experience where people can go and celebrate his legacy.

Discovering Bob Ross filmed in the underutilized property on the museum campus was serendipitous, says Jenkins. The museum, which already owned several Bob Ross works, was looking for ways to activate the space when they realized it was the modest origin of a man who touched millions of lives across the world. "To be able to put your feet in the same spot [where he painted] is really, really powerful," says Jenkins.

"Bob loved this house," says George Buss, vice president of visitor experience at Minnetrista. "[He] would take breaks from the filming to sit on the stairs to have an iced tea and think," and missed the home when the station moved to a larger space. "He would be tickled to know his story was being told inside of this humble space," says Buss, and that it has been a community effort to design the experience.

The museum has been working with the people who Bob Ross made a point to thank on every episode, including the director of *The Joy of Painting* as well as the camera people and staff who supported the show to feature their memories and voices in the experience.

The exhibit features a complete re-creation of the WIPB television studio where Bob Ross filmed *The Joy of Painting*, complete with his original easels, paint brushes, and palettes along with television cameras from that era, alongside some of his paintings on display. The fully interactive recreation has some items below glass, but others,

Above Bob filmed *The Joy of Painting* at WIPB-TV in Muncie, Indiana, in a home belonging to the Ball family (inventors of the Ball jar). In 2020, the Minnetrista Gathering Place in Muncie embarked on plans to renovate the building and create an interactive Bob Ross museum.

Above The Smithsonian Institution recently acquired several of Bob's paintings and artifacts, including his palette and brushes, for the permanent collection at the National Museum of American History.

such as stacks of fan mail, are available for visitors to touch. In one section, while *The Joy of Painting* plays on a monitor, attendees can step into Ross's place at the easel—an experience the *New York Times* reported left some visitors in tears.

That isn't all the Minnestrisa museum has planned. The next stage of the project will include the renovation of the second floor of the L.L. Ball house into a permanent painting workshop and gallery space dedicated to Bob Ross.

AT THE SMITHSONIAN

The Smithsonian acquired a number of original Bob Ross paintings and artifacts from his career, including his original easel made out of a converted step ladder, his painting equipment, and his notebooks, according to Eric Jentsch, curator of entertainment and sports at the National Museum of American History in Washington, D.C.

The institution also acquired fan letters, including some written after his passing, his brand merchandise, as well as an ammunition box from his Air Force drill sergeant days, an experience that led him to promise to never yell at anyone again and orient his life around peacefulness.

"We collected Bob Ross because we wanted both the entertainment story and his personal story," says Jentsch. "Our job is to talk about entertainment and pop culture that is important to American history, and to preserve artifacts."

He believes Bob Ross remains relevant because "he used television to educate and has an interesting business story. He didn't sell his paintings, but instead sold how to paint," says Jentsch. "He has become more influential and notable in the years after his passing, which is unusual in entertainment."

"When you look at the current media situation, there's a lot of argument, hot debate, and instant reactions," says Jentsch. "[Bob Ross represents] positivity, encouragement, peacefulness, all things I think younger people are drawn to because they are not getting it elsewhere."

In addition to the broader appeal of his philosophy, the museum acquired specific objects to represent the appeal Bob Ross had with more niche communities. For example, letters from "people who are going through adversity, like prisoners, where his process was beneficial to their lives," says Jentsch, or "people who have an ironic love of Bob Ross," who use merchandise representing his philosophy to develop their own identities.

A selection of these Bob Ross pieces, such as his easel, a painting with his iconic happy trees, and some brushes, will be featured in a new acquisitions exhibit once the museum has reopened post-COVID-19. Some of the other pieces will be later rotated through a larger, twenty-year exhibition on the history of entertainment in America.

EXPERIENCE BOB ROSS ANYWHERE

Although Bob Ross (and his work) has made his way into museums, he built his entire career creating virtual and community assets that are accessible for anyone to enjoy from their own homes and communities. In some ways, experiencing Bob Ross from your living room is the most authentic way to bring his lasting influence into your life.

"His gift was really reaching out through the TV and empowering each one of us to find the creativity within us," says Bracey.

Ross's philosophy is especially relevant in the wake of the global coronavirus crisis, when millions of humans were confined to their homes and restricted to virtual interactions. As the world seeks relief, searches for peace, and begins to process their frightening experiences, Bob Ross's ability to inspire hope, peace, and joy through virtual channels will continue to grow in value.

"His life message was about light" and creating peace in your world, says Buss, noting that painting was Bob Ross's venue to share a message that translates across mediums. "It was also about empowerment" to overcome fear that blocks creativity, which is critical in a world that needs as many people as possible to unleash that innate skill.

There are countless ways to be inspired by Bob Ross from your own home, starting with simply tuning in to old *The Joy of Painting* episodes. You can visit BobRoss.com, enter your zip code, and find screenings on television, or check out the Bob Ross

> "IT AWAKENS A DIFFERENT PART OF YOU, YOUR HEART AND YOUR SOUL AND YOUR BRAIN, BECAUSE YOU'RE HAVING A SHARED EXPERIENCE WITH OTHER PEOPLE." —ELIZABETH BRACEY

channel on YouTube to watch along on your computer.

If you'd like to practice painting along with Bob Ross while watching the show, you can order art supplies to your home and set up a living room art studio like the one at the exhibit in Muncie (sans the 1980s decor)—the tools and paints that Bob Ross used are available for sale on BobRoss.com, or you can get the same ones from your local craft store.

Even if you do not paint, you can bring his philosophy to your world by simply "experiencing art as much as you can in your own community," says Bracey. "It awakens a different part of you, your heart and your soul and your brain," she says, because you're "having a shared experience with other people." She recommends checking local galleries in your community, attending art shows at local high schools and colleges, and engaging in whatever formats people come together to celebrate creativity in your community.

ONE-STOP SHOP

Who knew you were able to replicate Bob Ross's iconic perm without going to the hairdresser, or add Ross's smile to a piece of toast? An investigation into the wacky (and fun!) merchandise available.

In 2018, Ryan Reynolds's *Deadpool 2* released a promotional teaser trailer featuring the titular character demonstrating a rather unique take on "Gettin' Wet on Wet" technique. It wasn't the first time Bob Ross would be parodied in pop culture, but it may have been the most outlandish to date.

Ross's publishing empire has a long tradition of producing wacky products, from unusual food products (pictured: an energy drink and a breakfast cereal) to garments with iconic paintings. As for more traditional merchandise, dozens of how-to books have been published, as well as titles for those more interested in immersing themselves in the philosophy of Bob Ross. You can re-create the show's hands-on experience with certified instructional books and DVDs featuring Bob Ross content that never aired, all available on BobRoss.com. *Be a Peaceful Cloud,* a collection of life lessons from Bob Ross (Universe, 2020), by Robb Pearlman is an easy way for a non-painter to embrace Ross's teachings.

Those interested in alternative or ironic ways of exploring Bob Ross can also pick up the Happy Little Accidents card game, or perhaps The Art of Chill board game, which combines Bob Ross quotes with creative exercises designed to be done with a group.

Of course, you could also just make a piece of toast.

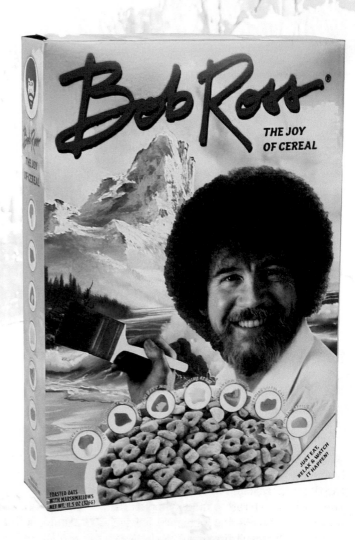

Celebrating His Life

by Nancy Lambert

As Bob Ross famously noted, "There's nothing in the world that breeds success like success." So it's no accident—happy or otherwise—that, decades after *The Joy of Painting* made him a beloved cultural icon, Ross's popularity continues to grow.

Legacy, as described in the hit Broadway musical, *Hamilton*, is "planting seeds in a garden you never get to see." That's a sentiment reminiscent of the folksy aphorisms Bob Ross often shared while painting on his show, *The Joy of Painting*, and a metaphor that a man known for his love of nature (almost as much as his signature perm) might have appreciated. In Ross's case, the "garden" is growing fast. Thanks to a combination of modern technology and evergreen messages of kindness and patience, Bob Ross is still inspiring, encouraging, and soothing, new generations of fans and artists twenty-five years after his passing.

When Ross died in 1995, the Internet as it is known today was just starting to sprout; sites like YouTube, Twitter, and Twitch were years, if not decades, away. Yet Ross didn't seed just a few niche online fandoms, instead, a digital empire flourished around his ethos, his voice, and his brand.

Launched in 2011, the Bob Ross channel on YouTube currently boasts over 4.5 million subscribers and more than 400 million views, while a Ross-dedicated subreddit, "Happy Trees," has offered "a place to share any content related to Bob Ross and The Joy of Painting!" to its 50,000 members for nearly a decade. Over on Ross's official Twitter account, @BobRossOfficial, more than 25,000 fans follow the account for pictures and inspirational quotes, and to keep up on the latest Bob Ross news of which there's more than you might expect, due in large part to Ross's overwhelming popularity on Twitch.

In 2015, Twitch, owned by Amazon and initially designed as a live video game streaming service, hosted an all-episode marathon of The Joy of Painting, drawing 5.6 million unique users—most under thirty-four years old—who immediately clamored for more Bob Ross. Ross's subsequent dedicated channel on Twitch quickly gained a large, devoted following, with 34 million views and more than 1.7 million followers. Ross's Twitch channel introduced a new generation to his easygoing demeanor and beginner-friendly technique by streaming original *The Joy of Painting* episodes—sometimes in

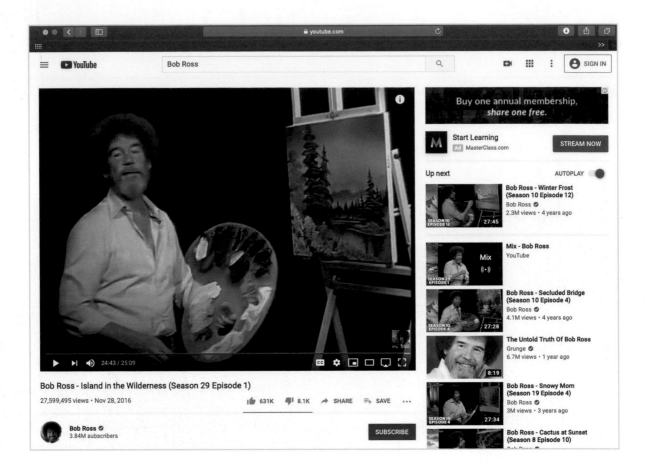

weekend-long marathons—alongside new content, including regular paint-alongs with Certified Ross Instructors (CRIs).

"I'd like to tell you that the phenomenal resurgence of Bob Ross in the last handful of years was because of some brilliant new marketing strategy on our part," says Joan Kowalski with a wink. "But honestly, all we did was let gravity take its course."

This surge in popularity with younger generations doesn't surprise CRI, Nic Hankins, who has hosted some of the "CRI Friday" paint-alongs on Twitch. He believes Ross's appeal is rooted in something deeper than art, "He just worked really hard at being who he was: an extremely patient and talented man with no trace of pretense, who simply wanted to share something he loved very dearly with the world. That sort of thing is absolutely timeless."

Of course, not everyone watching Ross's digital revolution is interested in painting.

Ross also gained a huge following in the ASMR community. As the phenomenon spills over into the mainstream, popular ASMR triggers also include just about any relaxing, soothing, or satisfying sounds or videos: a rug being power cleaned, soap being cut into tiny nuggets with a sharp blade, or someone squishing balls of colorful slime filled with sequins or beads (#crunchyslime).

Now, thanks to the broad availability of *The Joy of Painting* episodes online, Ross is a sensation (pun intended) in ASMR circles, where he frequently shows up on lists of common triggers (and in just about every trend piece on the subject). Ross's calming voice was a commodity long before streaming media, so much so that when Japanese media companies first explored syndicating *The Joy of Painting*, buyers eschewed dubbing it in Japanese, insisting on keeping the original audio with Ross's

own soft-spoken narration. As CRI Jeremy Rogers, notes, "Bob was the king of ASMR before that was even a thing."

But appreciation for Bob Ross isn't exclusive to the young and/or tingly, museums and arts centers are finally recognizing Ross's contributions with new exhibits and installations. Despite Ross's status as an established cultural phenomenon, until very recently, viewing an original Ross was nearly impossible (and forget about buying one, Bob Ross Inc. isn't selling). For years, the Bob Ross Art Workshop & Gallery in Florida housed one of the only publicly accessible displays of Ross's oil paintings, including landscapes from *The Joy of Painting*. Otherwise, Ross's substantial body of work—which he once estimated at 30,000 paintings—remained out of sight, with many Joy originals in storage at Bob Ross Inc.'s Virginia headquarters and others donated

to public television stations for use in fundraising efforts.

The surge in Ross's online popularity spurred interest in offline exhibitions. In 2019, Chicago's DePaul Art Museum featured four Ross paintings in *New Age, New Age: Strategies for Survival*, an exhibition which marked Ross's museum debut. That same year, the Franklin Park Arts Center in Virginia, with cooperation from Bob Ross Inc., presented twenty-four original Ross works in *Happy Accidents: An Exhibit of Bob Ross Paintings*, which also featured several CRI-led painting workshops. And at a later date, British Columbia's Penticton Art Gallery plans to exhibit thirty-two Ross originals—the largest showing of his work yet—in *Bob Ross: Happy Little Accidents*.

For a more immersive encounter, Ross fans are able to explore *The Joy of Painting*'s earliest roots in Minnetrista,

Above "I didn't understand the whole Bob Ross phenomenon until I started teaching," says Certified Ross Instructor Bernie Oropallo (in yelllow). "In my opinion, Bob Ross motivated more people to pick up a brush and paint than any other artist."

the arts and cultural center near where Ross first filmed his show. There, The Bob Ross Experience has opened Ross's original (and recently restored) Muncie, Indiana studio for tours, and displays a selection of his original artwork. Visitors are able to step into Ross's shoes at his easel in the fully interactive experience. Their museum will expand to include a permanent painting workshop and gallery space in the future.

Even the Smithsonian, an institution that Ross amicably quipped would "probably" never hang his art, recently acquired several of Ross's paintings—along with a selection of artifacts (including his palette and brushes) and fan memorabilia—for the National Museum of American History's permanent collection. The Smithsonian already hosted curator-led discussions about Bob Ross's

> "WITH ALL THE STRESSES IN OUR LIVES THESE DAYS, BOB ROSS IS JUST WHAT WE NEED." –JERRY SPENCE

legacy, calling *The Joy of Painting* "the most-recognized, most-watched television art show in history."

BOB'S PERM(ANENT) BRAND
Bob Ross knew the value of this kind of branding while he was alive—it's why he wouldn't change his hairstyle once he became known for it—so it makes sense that after his death, Bob Ross as a brand continues to be its own happy little stream, branching out in all sorts of interesting directions. In addition to the many nods and homages Ross receives within pop culture—from a faux *Family Guy* cameo to an Epic Rap Battle to a Google doodle feature—Ross's legacy (and likeness) lives on in a wide-ranging collection of licensed products.

Through Bob Ross Inc.'s careful management of Ross's image, both literal and figurative, his face and trademark halo of hair (even if he grew to loathe that perm) are as recognizable today as they were twenty-five years ago, if not more so.

In 2021, the seeds of Ross's legacy will take on a more literal meaning in southern Maryland, where Goldpetal Farms plans to

honor Bob Ross by making him the subject of their annual sunflower maze. In a twisting portrait spanning almost six acres, owner Jerry Spence and his team will create a massive labyrinth in the shape of Bob Ross's head. Even though this is the first time Goldpetal Farms is featuring a person as its maze, Spence is confident he can pull it off. "The image of Bob Ross is so well branded." Spence says, noting, "The hair will be a challenge, but who can honestly say that getting lost in Bob Ross's hair wouldn't be amazing? Nobody!"

In preparation for the maze, Spence and his team plant the sunflowers seeds in spring, then, when the plants are twelve inches tall, he marks and cuts the design. The field marking alone can take 75 hours. From start to finish, more than 250 hours of work, over several months, will go into the floral tribute, which, once completed, barely lasts a few weeks. "The flowers are rather fragile," says Spence, "and the season only lasts between 17 and 28 days." But the team at Goldpetal Farms believes Bob is worth the effort. "With all the stresses in our lives these days," Spence says, "Bob Ross is just what we need."

That's a sentiment embodied by the 3,000 Certified Ross Instructors who share Ross's technique—and perhaps more importantly, his famously encouraging demeanor—in classes and workshops around the globe. Representing Ross is a responsibility no CRI takes lightly. "The biggest challenge of being a CRI is to fill those big shoes that Bob left for us," says Nic Hankins.

As the Smithsonian recently noted on their site promoting a CRI workshop, Bob Ross "continues to open the world of painting to countless amateurs." Accordingly, many CRIs view the workshops they teach as a living legacy for Ross, honoring and continuing the positivity and kindness he shared in every episode of *The Joy of Painting*.

After teaching one of his classes with veterans, U.S. Air Force Staff Sergeant Robert Kingery, CRI, had an "eye-opening" realization, that "through me, Bob is still here and his ability to bring joy to others

lives on," he recalls. "I have the ability to make a difference through painting." Fellow CRI Faye Fletcher also believes that Ross's cultural significance does not reside solely on the canvas, "Some may say painting is his greatest legacy, but I think it's love."

ROSS'S LEGACY

That loving onscreen demeanor wasn't an act. In the documentary, *Bob Ross: The Happy Painter*, former *The Joy of Painting* production member Bill Bryant recalled, "The Bob that you see on the show is the Bob that we all knew, even behind the scenes." Jim Needham, the (now-retired) general manager of Ross's home station, thinks that Ross's authenticity is part of his appeal. "I think his sincerity came across, and I think people relate to that. They still relate to that." This might be the secret to why Ross's

popularity seems to be so enduring. As Bob Ross's longtime business partner and Bob Ross Inc. co-founder, Annette Kowalski, told the *New York Times* in an interview, "It's just never stopped. It just keeps going."

Whether he's inspiring new artists to pick up a brush and pursue the joy of painting, soothing an anxiety-riddled generation with his gentle voice, inspiring fans with long-ago quotes on a modern platform, or cheering someone's day from the side of a mug, it's clear that in the quarter century since his death, Ross's legacy has spread well past the confines of an ordinary garden. Perhaps the seeds of his legacy are growing into something more like one of his sprawling landscapes, only now it's up to Bob Ross's fans and followers to make sure that every happy little cloud, tree, and rock gets a friend.

Above Bob painted around 30,000 paintings over his lifetime. The National Museum of American History at the Smithsonian Institution recently acquired four of them.

Bob Ross

The Gallery

Instead of naming his paintings after a real locale, Bob Ross would focus on an idea—*Tranquil Wooded Stream or Golden Glow of Morning*—that evoked an emotional response in the viewer.

Light at the Summit (#J0P2904), 1993. The welcoming glow in the sky is reminiscent of Bob's last handful of paintings.

Misty Foothills (#J0P3006), 1994. Bob intended that the dark spot in the center of the painting at the base of the foothills suggests a walking path.

Trapper's Cabin (#JOP2908), 1993. This scene reflects Bob's experience living in Alaska, hiking and salmon fishing with his mother, Ollie.

Whispering Stream (#JOP0604), 1986. Bob used this painting to demonstrate how to create a scene that is in the painter's mind–not necessarily a real place.

Seaside Harmony (#JOP3010), 1994. Bob used only a painting knife to create the curling, crashing ocean to show how versatile the knife can be.

Tranquility Cove (#JOP3104), 1994. The intent of this piece was to create a painting with lots of warm colors that "will just make you feel good."

Winter's Grace (#JOP2809), 1993. Bob usually favored warm winter scenes. He painted this in response to fans who wanted to see a cold winter scene.

Covered Bridge (#JOP0306), 1985. This painting was inspired by the covered bridges Bob saw around Indiana.

The Old Mill (#JOP0309), 1985. This is the only painting Bob did that he realized wasn't going to be done in thirty minutes. He stopped filming and started again.

Evergreens at Sunset (#JOP0703), 1986. This departs from Bob's wet-on-wet technique. He liked to experiment, but was never very fond of this painting.

Misty Waterfall (#JOP0706), 1986. Bob frequently painted waterfalls, but they never lost popularity with his audience.

Northern Lights (#JOP0813), 1986. Bob experienced the bright dancing lights of the aurora borealis during his time in Alaska in the U.S. Air Force.

Deep Forest Lake (**#JOP1512**), **1989.** This painting started out with a black base around the edges—only the center was left white—to create a sense of depth.

Absolutely Autumn (**#JOP1802**), **1990.** Bob painted this in response to viewer requests to learn how to paint "great big, fluffy clouds."

Deep Woods (#JOP1607), 1989. Bob said of this painting: "Let's just do a beautiful little scene...that will make you happy."

Golden Morning Mist (#JOP1807), 1990. This was a replica of the painting that appeared in the opening of each episode of *The Joy of Painting*.

Majestic Peaks (#JOP1806), 1990. Bob created this painting for beginners. It includes all of the elements someone who had never held a paintbrush would need to learn.

MEREDITH PREMIUM PUBLISHING
Vice President & Group Publisher Scott Mortimer
Vice President, Group Editorial Director Stephen Orr
Vice President, Marketing Jeremy Biloon
Executive Publishing Director Megan Pearlman
Director, Brand Marketing Jean Kennedy
Associate Director, Brand Marketing Bryan Christian
Senior Brand Manager Katherine Barnet
Associate Director, Business Development and
    Partnerships Nina Reed

Editorial Director Kostya Kennedy
Creative Director Gary Stewart
Director of Photography Christina Lieberman
Senior Editor Alyssa Smith
Editorial Operations Director Jamie Roth Major
Manager, Editorial Operations Gina Scauzillo
Special thanks Brad Beatson, Samantha Lebofsky,
    Kate Roncinske, Laura Villano

MEREDITH NATIONAL MEDIA GROUP
President Catherine Levene
President, Meredith Magazines Doug Olson
President, Consumer Products Tom Witschi
President, Meredith Digital Alysia Borsa

EXECUTIVE VICE PRESIDENTS
Chief Revenue Officer Michael Brownstein
Digital Sales Marla Newman
Finance Michael Riggs
Marketing & Integrated Communications Nancy Weber

SENIOR VICE PRESIDENTS
Consumer Revenue Andy Wilson
Corporate Sales Brian Kightlinger
Research Solutions Britta Cleveland
Strategic Sourcing, Newsstand, Production Chuck Howell
Foundry 360 Matt Petersen
Product & Technology Justin Law

VICE PRESIDENTS
Finance Chris Susil
Business Planning & Analysis Rob Silverstone
Consumer Marketing Steve Crowe
Brand Licensing Toye Cody and Sondra Newkirk
Corporate Communications Jill Davison

Vice President, Group Editorial Director Stephen Orr
Chief Digital Content Officer Amanda Dameron
Director, Editorial Operations & Finance Greg Kayko

MEREDITH CORPORATION
Chairman & Chief Executive Officer Tom Harty
Chief Financial Officer Jason Frierott
Chief Development Officer John Zieser
Chief Strategy Officer Daphne Kwon
President, Meredith Local Media Group Patrick McCreery
Senior Vice President, Human Resources Dina Nathanson
Senior Vice President, Chief Communications Officer
    Erica Jensen

Vice Chairman Mell Meredith Frazier

WATERBURY PUBLICATIONS, INC.
www.waterburypublications.com
Creative Director Ken Carlson
Editorial Director Lisa Kingsley
Contributing Copy Editors Terri Fredrickson, Mike Olivo
Associate Art Director Doug Samuelson
Associate Editor Tricia Bergman
Senior Designer Mindy Samuelson
Assistant Editor William Bortz

"Dock Scene" by Bob Ross, Series 7, epi 12 (1986) – Big structures like this one enabled Bob to explain more fully to his audience exactly how to make buildings look realistic.

"I TRY TO GET PEOPLE TO BELIEVE IN THEMSELVES. I TELL PEOPLE, 'YOU CAN DO THIS.' AND THEY WRITE BACK AND SAY, 'YOU WERE RIGHT. I CAN DO THIS. AND NOW I BELIEVE I CAN DO ANYTHING.' AND THAT'S WHERE IT STARTS. YOU HAVE TO BELIEVE IN YOURSELF." –BOB ROSS